Peter Paul Rubens

Books
by
Samuel Edwards

PETER PAUL RUBENS

GEORGE SAND

VICTOR HUGO

THE DIVINE MISTRESS

BARBARY GENERAL: THE LIFE OF WILLIAM H. EATON

THEODORA

DAUGHTER OF GASCONY

FIFTY-FIVE DAYS AT PEKING

THE QUEEN'S HUSBAND

THE NAKED MAJA

THE TWISTED SABRE: A BIOGRAPHICAL NOVEL OF
BENEDICT ARNOLD

THE GENTLE FURY

THAT RANDALL GIRL

MASTER OF CASTILE

THE WHITE PLUME

THE DEVIL'S PRIZE

THE KING'S MESSENGER

THE SCIMITAR

Peter Paul Rubens

A Biography of a Giant

by
Samuel Edwards

DAVID McKAY COMPANY, INC.
New York

PETER PAUL RUBENS

For Paul Michael

LIBRARY OF CONGRESS CATALOG CARD NUMBER: 72–95157

PRINTED IN THE UNITED STATES OF AMERICA

Art is a shadow of Divine perfection.
—MICHELANGELO

I Perhaps no event in the late sixteenth century seemed less significant than the birth, on June 28, 1577, of the sixth child of Jan and Maria Pypelinckx Rubens, whom they named Peter Paul. Four of the older children were still living, and the harassed, impoverished parents, forced to dwell in exile far from their beloved Antwerp, did not rejoice.

Precisely where the infant was born was something of a mystery down to the present century. Antwerp long claimed the honor, and a bronze plaque attached to a modest house there proclaimed that it was the birthplace of the immortal Rubens. An almost identical plate could be found on a similar house in the city of Cologne, from which Jan Rubens was banned at the time, and a half-dozen other communities also insisted, but in vain, that Rubens had drawn his first breath within their town limits. There were endless rumors about other places, too, among them Madrid, Brussels, and Toledo, all of which had their champions, but none of which offered proof of their contention.

The truth of the matter is that Peter Paul Rubens came

into the world he was destined to conquer in the unprepossessing Westphalian town of Siegen, eighty kilometers west of Cologne. It was a dreary farmers' marketplace of about two thousand people and offered no attractions to a sophisticated couple. How Rubens' upper-middle-class Flemish parents happened to be there in the first place was a story that had scandalized, amused, and shocked every royal court in Europe—save one. The influence that incident and its long-lasting aftermath exerted on the great artist were so significant that his life can be understood only by looking into the past of his parents and of the great city that had been their home.

Jan and Maria Rubens were citizens of the Spanish Netherlands, the northern province ruled with an inflexible hand by the most unyielding and narrow-minded of the sixteenth century's many tyrants, Philip II. Even the most powerful of the nobles in the Lowland countries, William of Nassau, Prince of Orange, and the Counts Horn and Egmont, did not dare to raise their voices against him. It is small wonder that the head of the house of Orange was called William the Silent.

The Reformation had made only minor inroads into the Spanish Netherlands, and although there were many converts to Calvinism and the teachings of Luther, the Protestants were impotent. The harsh, intolerant spirit of the Inquisition was still all-pervading, and the Catholic bishops, most of them noble Spaniards appointed by Philip without prior consultation with the Pope, were the most powerful men in the land.

The royal regent, Margaret of Parma, was little more than a figurehead, and in 1566, when the Calvinists protested against their lot as second-class citizens by rioting, King Philip took charge of the situation himself. He sent the most hard-bitten of his generals, the Duke of Alba, into the province with troops drawn from Spain and Germany, and the rebellion was suppressed with a savagery unseen in northern Europe for centuries. Thousands died at the stake, were shot, or beaten to death; whole towns were gutted and destroyed, and the Counts Egmont and Horn were executed. The Prince of Orange was tempted to lead his subjects into battle against the "Spanish fury," but when he discovered that no other European rulers would support him, he discreetly went off to his estates in Germany to await a better day.

More than one hundred thousand Calvinists, liberals, Dutch and Flemish patriots, and even men who had been loyal to Spain but were suspected of harboring secret yearnings for independence, fled into exile. Among them were Jan and Maria Rubens, who took up residence in Cologne, near the castle of the Prince of Orange.

Jan Rubens was one of the most successful and respected members of the near-aristocracy in his native Antwerp, where his family had been prominent for more than two hundred and fifty years. The son of the city's leading apothecary, who owned a chain of shops in the Flemish capital, Jan Rubens had attended the universities of Louvain, Rome, and Padua, winning a degree as a doctor of law. In 1561, a few months after his marriage, the thirty-two-year-old attorney, who had already acquired a reputation as the best lawyer in the city, was appointed magistrate for the entire Antwerp district; he was allegedly the youngest man ever to hold that high a post.

Urbane, handsome, and clever, Jan Rubens was a product of the Renaissance—a nominal Catholic, whose travels had opened his mind to every field of learning, and a passionate believer in religious and political tolerance. He made no secret of his humanist views, freely expressing his opinions when he delivered his verdicts in court, and he acquired a name for himself as an advanced thinker, a high-principled jurist dedicated to learning and social improvement. Maria Pypelinckx was a fitting mate for a man of such great promise. The youngest and most beautiful of the three daughters of a prosperous Antwerp merchant and property owner, she was a decade younger than her husband. Educated at home by tutors, she was widely read and had traveled extensively; it is known that she visited London and Venice and twice made extended journeys to Madrid with her parents. It had long been a family joke that Maria was so idealistic it would be impossible to find a suitable husband for her. But her marriage to Jan Rubens appeared to be a perfect match, and the couple took an active part in the social life of Europe's most exciting city.

In the sixteenth century the capital of Flanders came into its own as the greatest seaport in Europe, and soon the arts would flower there in a cultural explosion rarely matched in history. Antwerp was the gateway to the Continent; her growing wealth was based on foreign trade that included the products of the Orient and the raw materials of the Americas, which Spain was exploiting with ruthless efficiency. The population had tripled in one hundred years, and at the time Peter Paul Rubens' parents were married the seaport had more than three-quarters of a million inhabitants and was still growing. Of all the Old World's cities only Paris and London were larger, and the walls surrounding the city, strengthened by stone forts, were extended so frequently that the never-ending building project was the subject of never-ending humor.

Like New York in a later era, Antwerp attracted so much money from trade that she became the banking capital of the Continent and was the world's leading commercial center. Merchants, bankers, and traders from every nation in Europe came to the city on business, and so many tongues were spoken there that it had become customary for schoolboys to learn a minimum of three or four languages. Her inns were the finest to be found anywhere on earth, and many of the hostels that catered to foreigners were as luxurious as palaces. Antwerp cooks were in demand at foreign courts, where it was taken for granted that anyone who had learned to prepare meals in Antwerp was familiar with the great dishes of many lands.

The city's position was due to her unique standing as the principal port of the Hapsburg family, one of whose branches ruled Spain, while the other, with Austria as its core, spread out across Germany and into Italy, and was still known as the Holy Roman Empire. Protected by special laws and granted unique privileges accorded to no other community by her authoritarian rulers, Antwerp gained such a predominant position as a business and financial center that she was as indispensable to the French, the British, and the Portuguese as she was to the Spaniards and the Austrians. It was said that she was visited each year by fifty thousand foreign merchants, traders, and bankers who contributed their share to her annual income of 3 billion gold francs, a sum greater than the combined gross business of London, Paris, Venice, and Antwerp's nearby rival, Bruges.

There was no manufacturing in the city, which contributed little of her own merchandise to the world, and this was a blessing to the good burghers who required continuing peace if they were to remain prosperous. The lower class was exceptionally docile, and the ferment of the Renaissance that transformed other major cities into brawling centers of social discontent was virtually unknown. The dock workers, sailors, bargemen, and warehouse employees enjoyed the highest wages paid anywhere on earth to the proletariat, which enabled them to live in comfortable homes, to afford good food and clothing, and to send their children to the only schools for the masses to be found anywhere on the Continent.

Antwerp's absentee masters, including the myopic Philip himself, were just barely intelligent enough to allow nothing to interfere with the golden flow that enriched their empire. Any foreign merchant who had been issued a valid passport for a visit to Antwerp was immune from arrest under any circumstances; if he committed a crime, he was handed over to the legation of his own country, and if he was guilty of fraud or other chicanery in business, his passport was taken from him. This drastic punishment was universally regarded as so severe that a visitor, if no more honest than his neighbor, went to great pains to avoid detection. Criminals from other parts of Europe and even men who had prices on their heads as traitors were free to live openly in Antwerp, where they could walk through the tree-lined, cobbled streets without fear—provided they could prove to Jan Rubens and his fellow magistrates that they were engaged in a legitimate enterprise, contributing to the prosperity and stability of the city.

Perhaps the most extraordinary of the laws governing Antwerp was that her citizens paid no taxes to either the state or the Church. Every permanent resident was expected to make a voluntary annual contribution to the Spanish crown, and the wealthy, hoping to preserve this status of heaven on earth, were so generous that no serious attempt was made to exact tribute from those who were not in a financial position to give. A similar freedom from taxation was granted to every foreigner who did business in Antwerp, and by the middle of the sixteenth century the city had become the most flourishing free port on earth.

Commercial fairs were held for three-week periods four times each year, when the seasons changed, and so many visitors came to town for these occasions that even the wealthy were expected to provide lodgings for those who sought accommodations. The Church, which benefitted from the gifts of the rich, receiving 50 percent of every contribution, was as accommodating as the state, and suspended excommunications and interdictions during commercial fairs. The bishops, of whom there were no fewer than five in the district, remained carefully unaware of the existence of the luxurious brothels and gaming houses that catered to the visitors; and the owners of these establishments found ways to express their financial gratitude for the policy of ignorance.

This tolerance did not apply to the residents of Antwerp, however, and the good burghers were pleased to live their private lives apart from the strangers in their midst. Even a small merchant was wealthy by the standards of other places, and he allowed nothing to interfere with his continuing ability to make money. His sons were trained to enter the family business; his wife and daughters were protected from the roving eyes of visitors; and although an outsider might be invited to dine at a man's home, the family was never present on these occasions. Antwerpers were moral men, and although they didn't care if strangers enjoyed drinking and wenching, they maintained their own standards with middle-class zeal.

It was inevitable, however, that the presence of so many foreigners from so many lands should influence the thinking of Antwerp's citizens. Although they failed to realize it themselves, they were far more tolerant of alien ideas and customs than the people of any other city in Europe. They were exposed to other cultures, to new concepts, to strange philosophies; even the ways of Islam, brought by traders from the Ottoman Empire, found acceptance. Personal liberty was the right of every man, and if the native elected to live morally and prudently, the choice was his own.

A community crisscrossed by countless canals, Antwerp became known as the Venice of the north and, in many ways, became as Italian in appearance and outlook as the great Adriatic port. The basic architecture was Flemish Gothic, to be sure, but Italian influences were felt as early as 1521, when Herman and Domien de Waghemakers designed the tower and spire of the Church of Notre-Dame. The old Exchange building, the commercial heart of the city, was given a new façade, as was the Van Liere Palace, which the Emperor Charles V had used as his headquarters on his frequent visits to Antwerp. A new industry came into being—that of making altarpieces and other church ornamentation—and these objects were as Italian-inspired as those produced by rival companies in Milan and Florence.

The architectural masterpiece of the era—the new town hall, which was designed and built by Cornelius de Vriendt—used the old Flemish style as its base but was completely Italian in spirit by the time the architect was finished. Started in 1561, the building was completed three years later, and even now, after four centuries, it is regarded as the finest example of Renaissance work in Flanders. But as Peter Paul Rubens himself would demonstrate so conclusively, visits to Italy and the influence of Italian artists in no way detracted from the purely Flemish inspiration of the Antwerp artist. The roots of his own heritage were too deep and strong to be diminished by the spirit or style imported from other places.

Nowhere was this seen more clearly than in the social life of the Antwerp merchant and his family. The wealthy citizen might own the property on which an expensive brothel was located, and thanks to his status it was exempt from taxation. But he and his sons never frequented the establishment, although he might send a foreign client there as his guest. Visitors crowded into gaming houses, and card-playing became popular with the aristocrats and middle class of Antwerp, but they played only with friends in their own homes. Under no circumstances would a respectable Antwerp matron be seen dining in a public inn, but she made certain that the meals prepared under her own roof were prepared with the spices and condiments of the East that contributed so much to the city's prosperity.

8

The ladies wore gems and gowns of rich cloth imported by their husbands from distant places. They gave dinners and held musical evenings, they graced assemblies and balls, but only a handful of outsiders ever saw them there. The women of Antwerp became renowned as the legendary beauties of Europe and were surrounded by something of an aura of mystery because so few foreigners met or consorted with them. Fathers made certain their daughters' dowries were not dissipated by pleasure-loving husbands from France, Germany, or Spain; and saw to it that a prospective son-in-law was a member in good standing of a solid Antwerp family.

By the time Antwerp reached the climax of her glory, at about the time Jan and Maria Rubens were married, the city had developed an unerring instinct for making money in new ways. The wealthy members of the middle class were imitating the great nobles of Europe by purchasing paintings, statues, and other works of art, and the custom spread quickly across the Continent. The demand for art being greater than the supply, Antwerp trained her own artists; and hundreds, perhaps as many as two thousand, were members of the Guild of St. Luke, which had been formed in the fourteenth century.

Members were divided into four categories, each of which had its own organization within the guild. The painters were the most numerous, followed by the sculptors; in third place were the printers, who produced more books than were published in any other European city. The wood carvers constituted the smallest group, with as few as fifty to sixty members. Since it was customary for men to follow in the vocational footsteps of their fathers, a great many Flemish artists were the sons and grandsons of artists.

The painter or sculptor was generally regarded as an artisan rather than a member of a profession, and most were content with their middle-class standing. Churches in every part of Europe were commissioning works of art, wealthy citizens of Antwerp itself were filling every room in their homes with paintings and statues, and the demand was so great that the Guild of St. Luke changed its rules. A man was required to spend only five years as an apprentice, instead of the seven years that had been customary for generations, and then to become a journeyman for a period of three years, instead of five, before being awarded his certificate as a master. The pressure continued to increase, and by the time of Peter Paul Rubens, prior to the end of the sixteenth century, the entire journeyman status was abandoned, thus enabling an artist to strike out on his own still more quickly.

One reason for this revolutionary change was the impatience of youth to share in the wealth that came to Antwerp from every corner of the world. The commercial rulers of the city were far younger than the leaders of the business communities of other metropolitan centers, and it was said that any merchant, banker, or trader worth his salt could retire by the time he reached forty. The heads of most business houses, in 1561, were in their thirties, and four major concerns boasted managing directors not yet out of their teens.

Few couples enjoyed life in Antwerp more than did the dashing Jan Rubens and his lovely bride. He had acquired a reputation as a ladies' man, but his marriage apparently sobered him, and he was faithful to the wife whom he escorted with obvious pride to scores of social functions. Not many had as wide a circle of friends as the brilliant magistrate and his equally bright Maria, and both found favor at the court of the Archduke Albert and Archduchess Isabella, who would succeed Margaret of Parma as co-regents.

Wise men began to wonder if life in the earthly Eden would remain unchanged forever, and a few could see dark clouds on the horizon. As early as 1566 the economy of Spain and her neighbor Portugal began to decline, in the main because both freely spent the wealth of their colonies while producing nothing themselves. The financial recession that had started there spread by the following year to the rest of Europe, and for the first time in a century and a half Antwerp began to feel the pinch.

The rich remained relatively untouched, but the poor, as usual, were the first to suffer, and the Calvinists expressed their discontent by rioting and holding unprecedented demonstrations in the streets. Every man of substance knew that the Spanish crown could not tolerate such insubordination, which would have to be punished to halt the spread of revolution.

No one, however, anticipated the severity of the Duke of Alba's counterattack. Antwerp was his primary target, but he took his time marching to the city, halting to sack and burn many smaller towns before bringing the terror to the heart of Flanders. Some of Antwerp's nobles and leading merchants did not believe that Alba would destroy the source of so much income, but Jan Rubens knew better and fled with his wife and four children to Amsterdam, where they remained for a short time. There were four children in the family: Jan-Baptiste, born in 1562; Blandine, born in 1564; Claire, born in 1565; and Hendrik, born in 1567. Another child, Bartholomeus, died in infancy, and yet another son, Philip, would join the family in 1574, prior to the birth of Peter Paul in 1577.

The tidal wave of the "Spanish fury" was so great that little is known about the refugees from the Duke of Alba's wrath during the next two years, and little can be said with certainty about the Rubens family prior to 1570 other than that they wandered from place to place in search of a permanent home. Certainly few literate men remained alive in Antwerp to record the damage there. At least ten thousand intellectuals, bankers, merchants, and community leaders were put to death, and according to some estimates the death toll may have been closer to fifty thousand. Spanish and German troops, allowed to run wild, sacked, raped, and pillaged at will, leaving the crippled city in ruins—and creating a completely united will to resist on the part of the Flemish people and their cousins, the Dutch.

Jan and Maria Rubens heard tales of horror from friends who were fortunate enough to escape from the Spaniards, but the Rubens family was far from the scene of the atrocities, having arrived in Cologne in 1572 because Jan had an opportunity to find gainful employment there. He didn't yet know it, but he was leaping from the frying pan into the center of a different sort of fire.

II William I of the Netherlands —Prince of Orange, Duke of Flanders, Count of Nassau, and Viscount of Antwerp, known to posterity as William the Silent—was the patient statesman, cunning diplomat, and almost unbelievably gallant warrior who succeeded in winning the freedom of his domain from Spanish rule and establishing the Netherlands as an independent nation. Short and slender, with a neat beard, black hair, and dark, piercing eyes, he pursued his goal with a single-minded zeal that made day-to-day living difficult for his closest associates. He buried three wives, then took a fourth, and members of his entourage knew that all four had found it difficult to love a patriot and hero who devoted his entire being to his sacred cause.

Long a widower for the first time, he made his second marriage in 1561, the same year Jan and Maria Rubens were married. William was nominally a Catholic, although at heart he was a liberal and disciple of Erasmus, the great humanist; and his bride was a Protestant princess, Anne, the seventeen-year-old daughter of the Elector Maurice of Saxony. Some romantic historians of the nineteenth century

13

credited Anne with arousing William's sympathy for his Lutheran subjects, but no valid evidence exists to indicate that she exerted any influence over William in either his personal or official life.

Anne's only claim to fame at the time of her marriage was her beauty, and she deserved the praise she won as the loveliest princess in Europe. She was slightly taller than her husband, with a willowy figure far more slender than that which was considered attractive in the Netherlands and Flanders. She had long, blond hair, enormous blue eyes, and a perpetual pout that appeared in every painting and sketch made of her by artists of the period. From the outset, her marriage was far from idyllic, thanks to her husband's preoccupation with the political problems caused by the Spanish crown; and when he refused to take an oath of fealty to the Duke of Alba in 1568, she fled with him into exile.

William's Netherlands possessions were confiscated, although Philip II did not deprive him of his titles, for fear of setting a precedent that might cause troubles for various members of the Hapsburg clan at some future date. William still owned his castle in Cologne, as well as numerous other properties, however; and after suffering a defeat in 1569, when he first tried to meet Alba in the field, he traveled incessantly throughout Europe in an attempt to establish the coalition that would enable him, in 1572, to take the field again.

The independently wealthy Anne was left behind in the cold, gloomy castle in Cologne, where she was surrounded by a miniature court of Dutch and Flemish women and old men, the younger and more vigorous of William's followers being occupied elsewhere on his behalf. Badly spoiled and demanding the attention she had enjoyed all her life, Anne led a lonely, miserable existence. She took no interest in politics and had always been so sheltered that the horrors inflicted on her husband's Dutch and Flemish subjects were beyond her grasp. She needed love, and according to persistent rumors emanating from her little court, she took it wherever she found it.

It may or may not be true that she engaged in many affairs, but only three during the period from 1568 to 1570 have been authenticated. A young officer who served William as a junior aide-de-camp was the first, but he was killed in action in the campaign against the Duke of Alba. The second was the son of a Cologne banker, and the third was the banker himself. Letters concerning her infidelity were sent to William by some of the good ladies of Anne's court, but the Prince of Orange found it more convenient to ignore them than to take action. He was spending his energy, time, and personal fortune in a gargantuan effort to unite and free his subjects from a tyrant, and he had no heart for a personal scandal that might rob him of support in some of Europe's wealthier and more powerful courts. Even if Anne was being unfaithful to him, she was discreet, and only a few people knew of her supposed affairs; he decided to deal with her at some later time when he could better devote himself to the problem.

It was at this juncture, in the summer of 1570, that Jan Rubens was introduced to the little court by a fellow refugee who was recommending him as the assistant manager of Princess Anne's estate. Jan was forty-one, but he was lean after his wanderings with his wife and small children and had lost none of his personal charm. Ladies at the court who had known him when he had been Antwerp's principal magistrate still found him irresistible, and Anne of Saxony shared their opinion. Jan Rubens was hired as legal counsel and assistant financial adviser to Princess Anne and soon became chief financial adviser, his predecessor having been sent into retirement when he and Anne started their tumultuous affair.

Maria and the Rubens children had taken up residence in a small house in Cologne, but Jan was required to spend most of his time at the castle owned by William of Orange; and as his affair progressed, he rarely came home. According to the most popular of the stories about Maria Pypelinckx, she knew nothing of the liaison, but when the storm broke over her husband's head she stood loyally at his side. Other accounts indicate that this intelligent, sensitive woman could not have remained ignorant of the situation but closed her eyes to it, with or without her husband's knowledge. It has even been said that she connived with him until he won Anne's favor, but this may be going too far since Maria was a woman of great integrity.

The facts of the situation cannot be denied. A former magistrate, once a prosperous and honored citizen of Antwerp, was a refugee who had a wife and four children to feed. He not only earned his pay at the royal court but performed personal services for a dissolute princess that guaranteed he would continue to be paid the money that supported his family. Maria Pypelinckx was a sensible woman and a realist, who knew her dream of returning to Antwerp would not be fulfilled for a long time, so she well may have known of her husband's affair.

If she knew, she undoubtedly realized, as he did, that he was flirting with a fate as dangerous as any the Duke of Alba might have devised for a suspected Flemish dissident. It was an unwritten but firm rule that any man—noble or commoner—who made a cuckold of the head of a royal household would be punished with death by hanging. So Jan Rubens faced the scaffold if his liaison with Anne of Saxony was discovered.

But the Prince of Orange was too busy raising an army and finding the funds for arms, supplies, and uniforms for his growing force; he absented himself from Cologne for a year, which stretched out to eighteen months, then two years. The lovers became increasingly careless, and to the dismay of the ladies who constituted Anne's court, they even went off for days at a time to a private chalet the princess owned in the forest near the town of Siegen, a full day's ride from Cologne.

Prince William was duly informed of his wife's latest infidelity, but again he chose to say and do nothing. He was on the verge of starting his great campaign to evict the foreign tyrant from his beloved Netherlands, and anything that distracted him from that effort might prove fatal to his cause. Thus he sent word to Anne through one of his brothers, Count John of Nassau, whose Puritanism was typical of the rigid morality of Cologne, to cease her affair and dismiss her lover; having given the order, he put the matter out of his mind.

But Anne of Saxony was as foolish as she was pretty, and Jan Rubens was either stupidly bewitched by her or was given no voice in the matter by an imperious princess. The affair went on. Then in the spring of 1572—according to some accounts it was the spring of 1571, but the precise dates were smudged by supporters of the House of Orange —Anne of Saxony discovered she was pregnant.

Since Prince William had not seen his wife in almost two years, under no circumstances could he have been the father. The story of Anne's infidelity could be kept secret no longer, and soon every court in Europe heard the news. Courtiers snickered in private, but their expressions were grave in the presence of solemn monarchs who believed, with justice, that the cause of monarchy had been damaged everywhere, and at a time when rebels in many lands were attacking the entire political system.

Count John of Nassau was forced to act swiftly on his brother's behalf, and one morning as Jan Rubens left the house of his wife and children after a visit of a few days, troops in the service of Count John placed him under arrest and confined him in the dungeon of the castle in which he had dared to bed the princess.

The response of Maria Pypelinckx to her husband's crisis was magnificent and was preserved for posterity in several letters. One was ostensibly addressed to her husband, but she hoped it would be seen by Count John and members of his entourage, if not by Prince William himself. In it she said:

> I am sure that if these good gentlemen saw my tears they would pity me, even if they were made of wood or stone; so when no other course is left to me, that is the one I shall follow, even though you have written to me with instructions not to resort to entreaties. I shall ask every gentleman of influence and power to assist me and my children in our hour of extremity. More than that, if it should be possible, I shall go myself to His Highness of Orange and beg him for mercy on your behalf.
>
> Aye, I appeal to One who stands above even the greatest of kings and princes, and I beg Almighty God to help me, addressing him thusly: "You do not desire the death of a sinner, but rather that he should turn from his wickedness and live. Imbue the souls of these good gentlemen, whose anger we have provoked, with Thine Own spirit of mercy, that we may shortly be delivered from this terror and desolation."
>
> I will offer my most heartfelt prayers for you, my beloved husband, and our children will do as I do; these poor little ones send you their love and long to see you—and so do I, God knows!
>
> Written on the first day of April, between midnight and one o'clock in the morning. And you must not again call yourself "your unworthy husband," for I have already forgiven you everything. In my sight and in my heart you are blameless.

18

The letter was the opening salvo in a campaign to save her husband's life, and Maria Pypelinckx undoubtedly realized that her own dramatic gesture of forgiveness could not fail to impress Count John—or Prince William himself if he had time to read what she had written. But the authorities replied by transferring the prisoner to a more secure dungeon, located in the bowels of the castle of Dillenburg, another property owned by William of Orange.

On three separate occasions Maria is known to have visited the dungeon, but on each she was denied access to her husband and told nothing regarding his mental or physical condition. She had no idea whether he was in good health, whether his guards starved him, or whether he was being subjected to torture. The honor of the House of Orange was at stake, and Count John, who had not read the works of Erasmus with the avidity his brother had displayed, was renowned for his hot temper and cruel streak.

Historical detectives, who have inclined toward the belief that Maria Pypelinckx may have known of her husband's affair and even encouraged it for the sake of her family's financial security, have pointed to one significant phrase in her letter to her husband. She spoke of the gentlemen "whose anger *we* have provoked," and certainly it is possible to interpret her words as a sharing of her husband's guilt. But it is impossible to determine whether she meant the phrase literally or as a figure of speech.

Regardless of the degree of her own involvement, she made almost superhuman efforts on Jan Rubens' behalf. Through relatives in Antwerp who had not offended the forces of occupation, she obtained a travel visa for her husband's half-brother, Philip de Lantmeter, who had been a boyhood schoolmate of Count John's. De Lantmeter came to Cologne and, accompanied by Maria, was received by the brother of the Prince of Orange, who emulated William the Silent by making no comment whatever after listening to their pleas.

Soon thereafter a lack of funds forced Maria to give up her house and move in with a cousin, a Cologne apothecary named Raymond Ringott. At about this same time the municipal authorities of the city, embarrassed by the presence in their midst of the wife and children of the man who had been Anne of Saxony's lover, took deportation proceedings against her. Maria had literally no place to go and fought hard against the order, which was suddenly and inexplicably dismissed.

It appears that influence was used on her behalf, but nothing is known about these efforts. According to one account that has persisted for more than four hundred years, Count John of Nassau intervened and caused the Cologne officials to change their minds. This raises the question of why the brother of William the Silent would have exerted himself for Jan Rubens' wife.

There are two possibilities. According to one, the count and his brother were trying to present a sympathetic image to the world that would emphasize their humanity and point up the cruelty of the Spaniards in the Low Countries. The mere fact that Anne of Saxony's lover had a charming wife and several small children would be of help in winning support from rulers who thought the Spaniards were going too far in suppressing the dissidents of Flanders and the Netherlands. If this theory is valid, Prince William or his brother had already decided that Jan Rubens should be given some punishment short of execution.

The other possibility seems farfetched in the light of Maria Pypelinckx's behavior over a period of many years. According to this notion, she gave herself to Count John in return for his help. On reflection this story is not as ludicrous as it first appears to be, since it is known that Maria did establish some sort of personal relationship with Count John and that this acquaintanceship extended over a period of many years. Some of Peter Paul Rubens' early biographers advanced the possibility that he might have been sired by Count John, and as will be seen, their arguments carry some weight.

In any event, Maria Pypelinckx was permitted to remain in Cologne and continued to carry on her unremitting campaign to win her husband's freedom. Anne of Saxony had retired to her lodge near Siegen, and in August she gave birth to a daughter. Had the child been a son, he would have caused complications in the line of succession of the royal houses of Orange and Saxony, and there can be little question that Jan Rubens would have been executed without delay in order to make certain that Anne's son carried a bastard's brand.

The fact that the baby was a girl gave Maria new hope that her husband's life would be spared, and she obtained permission—again in some mysterious way—to pay a visit to the princess. Romantic German poets and playwrights have made the confrontation between the two women the core of a number of works of art, but they were relying exclusively on their own imaginations. It is unfortunate that not one authentic word about the meeting of Jan Rubens' wife and his royal mistress was reduced to paper and survived.

Presumably Maria sought Anne's assistance for Jan, but the princess was in no position to ask her preoccupied husband for mercy, and it is unlikely that she would have gone to his brother, who is known to have hated her. No information is available, either, on whether Maria saw the infant her husband had sired. Whatever may have happened at the lodge near Siegen, nothing concrete came of the meeting, and the unhappy wife was forced to resume her virtually hopeless campaign.

Time was on her side, however. Prince William continued to procrastinate, Count John was reluctant to have Jan Rubens executed without a specific order to that effect from his brother, and in the meantime the continuing imprisonment of Jan Rubens was a never-ending reminder to the world of the humiliation the house of Orange had suffered. Finally, in the late summer of 1573, Maria received word that she would be granted a reunion with her husband in Siegen; presumably she assumed that he would be granted a brief holiday from prison for the purpose.

When she reached the town, she found no quarters available, so she lodged at the small local inn. Probably she soon discovered that Princess Anne was no longer in residence at her lodge but had gone elsewhere under heavy guard. Unable to rent a house, the stubborn Maria nevertheless obtained the rental of a plot of unused ground near the town walls and planted a number of vegetables there. If her wait for her husband was protracted, at least she and her children would have something to eat. The suspicion arises that she was making a deliberate play for Count John's sympathy since the season was already too far advanced for planting.

Then, out of the blue, Jan Rubens arrived in Siegen unannounced and seemingly a free man. The exact date is unknown, and no information has been discovered regarding his physical or mental health. The conditions under which he had been released were severe: He had been forced to pay bail of six thousand gold thalers, a staggering sum which he had borrowed from friends and relatives still in Antwerp, and this sum would be forfeited if he violated his parole in any way; he was obliged to return to his cell if summoned; and he was permitted to establish a residence in the countryside near Siegen, but under no circumstances could he pass the walls and enter the town itself. Also, he was forbidden to attend church services or step inside a house of God for any purpose, and he was directed to remain, at all times, within two kilometers of his dwelling. A representative of the house of Orange would visit him regularly and was empowered to send him back to prison if he disobeyed a single directive.

In spite of the restrictions, however, Jan and Maria Rubens were reunited, and there was a chance they could begin a new life, even though subsequent events demonstrated that the man's spirit was broken. Maria Pypelinckx borrowed money from relatives in Antwerp and Cologne, and the family rented a modest house in the woods outside the Siegen town walls.

Life could not have been easy for the family. The townspeople avoided Jan Rubens; few people spoke to his wife when she went to the town market to buy food. Because their sons were mocked when they attended school, the beleaguered couple tutored them at home. It is no exaggeration to say the entire family lived in total isolation, and Maria obtained some measure of relief only when she and her children attended church.

A sudden crisis arose when Count John of Nassau received a report to the effect that Jan Rubens had violated his parole by going into Siegen. Pending an investigation of the charge, Rubens was confined to his house. The former magistrate wrote a long brief in his own defense, but the effort was feeble, demonstrating that he had not yet recovered his spirit. He was saved from further imprisonment only because Maria also wrote to the count, swearing an oath to the effect that her husband had been at home with her and their children at the time he allegedly had been seen in Siegen.

The charges were dropped, but Maria again had to write to Count John to ask that her husband's privilege of walking in the countryside be restored. Her request was granted, but the count rejected a second request. Under no circumstances, he wrote, would Jan Rubens be permitted to set foot inside a church—Roman Catholic or Protestant.

The culprit's situation was far from hopeless, however.

Maria learned from relatives in Cologne that Princess Anne had been returned to her family in Saxony and had been sent into seclusion at a remote castle. There she remained, increasingly forgotten by the world she had scandalized, until her premature death in 1577. Two sketches of her made in the last year of her life by unknown artists indicate that she had aged almost beyond recognition.

On April 24, 1574, Maria Pypelinckx Rubens gave birth to a son, who was named Philip. Her reconciliation with her husband was complete and must have stopped stories to the effect that she was merely going through the motions of a renewed marital relationship in order to win sympathy for herself.

Soon after, the first positive change brightened the lives of the unhappy family. Spain graciously restored the property of those whose possessions had been confiscated in Antwerp, once again under Spanish rule. Jan Rubens once again owned his house and its furnishings, as well as other real estate and his financial interest in two trading houses that were continuing to be profitable. Maria's ownership of a half-dozen houses in Antwerp, which she had inherited from her father, was restored. The stroke of a pen in Madrid made the poverty-stricken family solvent.

Jan Rubens received permission to go into Cologne long enough to sign papers granting his wife a power of attorney and began to look forward to happier days. With funds again available, Maria Pypelinckx applied to Count John for permission to move into some portion of the Low Countries that had already been freed by William of Orange in his increasingly successful campaign against the Spanish tyrant. The count's reply was succinct: Mrs. Rubens and her children were free to live where they pleased in lands controlled by the House of Orange, but Jan Rubens would remain outside Siegen. The quasi-prisoner's basic situation was unchanged.

to another assertion, which cannot be dis-
ntly, Peter Paul Rubens was the son of Maria
nly placed nobleman, perhaps Count John of
n the little that is known of the devout, hard-
ia Pypelinckx's life it is doubtful that she retali-
her husband by committing adultery, but there
s in the life of the young Rubens that have
explained. At the age of ten he obtained a
he household of a great lady; this position never
been open to the child of a middle-class family
ary circumstances. Maria engaged in a lifelong
r money, yet her youngest never lacked funds
imes was expensively dressed.
xuries may have been no more than maternal
es, special treatment accorded the baby of a
t had fought long and hard to overcome the
osed on them by Jan Rubens' behavior. As to the
lationship that Peter Paul Rubens enjoyed with
roughout his entire life, mingling with the mem-
any of Europe's ruling families, there could be a
planation. Certainly it is possible that even those
e the purple were not blind to his extraordinary
hen the rest of the civilized world was hailing his
Therefore, until such time as solid evidence is pre-
o the contrary, it must be assumed that Peter Paul
son of Jan and Maria Rubens.
ertain, too, that he enjoyed no normal childhood.
d Philip, who was three years his senior, were
d by the older children of the family in a conspiracy
ce, and neither of the small boys ever heard a word
heir father's disgrace. Certainly Jan Rubens did not
n it, but there is a brief reference in a letter that
wrote to Peter Paul, when both were men, indicating
eir father often sat them on his lap and told them of
fferings of the Flemish people during the years of the
ish fury."

Two events of lasting significance occurred within three months of each other in 1577, and the first of them attracted the attention of the entire civilized world. Prince William of Orange emerged the victor in his long struggle against his nation's oppressors, and Spain signed a peace treaty granting the Netherlands complete freedom. Flanders would remain under nominal Spanish control, but all rights of her citizens were restored, and the province would enjoy special privileges unknown in other portions of Spain's empire. The treaty was signed in March, and bonfires were lighted everywhere in Europe.

On June 28 of the same year Maria Pypelinckx Rubens gave birth to her sixth child, an event that went unnoticed and was recorded in no church registry. The baby was named Peter Paul, and his prospects in life seemed dismal.

III The earliest years in the life of
Peter Paul Rubens were still
exceptionally trying for his
parents and his brothers and
sisters, but he was too young to
know what was happening in
the world around him. The first major improvement came
late in 1578, when the baby was a year and a half old. The
victorious William of Orange could afford to be generous;
Anne of Saxony was dead, and the world was forgetting the
existence of former lawyer Jan Rubens. So the semi-pris-
oner was permitted to leave territory controlled by Count
John, although he was expressly forbidden to return to
Flanders or set foot on any soil under the direct jurisdiction
of Prince William.

Early in 1579 the family returned to Cologne, where Jan,
with the help of relatives and friends, resumed his law
practice. Since it was obvious that he would be unable to
earn a living for a time, the ever-resourceful Maria opened
a rooming house, which, thanks to her competent management, flourished from the outset. Eventually her husband
built a practice of respectable proportions, which enabled
him to hold his head somewhat higher, but at no time did

26

he win social
refugees and n

Virtually noth
his parents durin
in later years ind
mother, admired
toward her. At n
father other than t
Rubens had been
as an attorney in
"Spanish fury."

The mature Rub
sure, and some aut
always claimed he
assertion may have b
wanted to bury any
unpleasantness conne

Actually, no one kr
bens was born in Siege
in only one source, a pl
in 1649, nine years af
Antwerp. No mention
the baptismal records of
of any city or town.

This lack of documenta
for the rumors regarding
may be dismissed without
ted he was secretly the ch
Saxony, and that Maria Pyp
and pretended he was her
band further punishment. T
cess Anne had long been
under the watchful eye of S
after his release from prison
except his own wife and chil

27

According
missed as lig
and of a hig
Nassau. Fro
working Ma
ated against
are mysteri
never been
position in
would have
under ordi
struggle fo
and at all

These l
indulgence
family tha
stigma im
special re
royalty th
bers of
simple e
who wo
talents
genius.
sented
was the

It is
He an
shielde
of sile
about
menti
Philip
that t
the s
"Spa

The impression these tales made on a sensitive and imaginative boy may have been Peter Paul's single greatest heritage from his father. Certainly they would help explain the lyricism, romantic yet tragic, that appeared so often in the work of the mature Rubens.

If some faint spark of a yearning for adventure still flickered somewhere deep within the tired soul of Jan Rubens, his youngest child may have sensed it. If so, the communication of that desire offers some explanation of a trait that distinguished Peter Paul from his siblings. Without exception, they were solid, dull, and respectable middle-class Flemings who shunned the limelight and lived quietly. But Peter Paul was flamboyant, courted fame, and rarely missed an opportunity for adventure, even when it meant neglecting the vocation he loved with such passion.

Little data concerning the early boyhood of Peter Paul has ever been discovered, other than the fact that he and Philip were tutored at home by a father whose unsuccessful practice of law gave him ample time to teach his sons Latin and Greek, the classics, mathematics, and the foundations of Spanish, French, and English. Flemish was spoken at home, and Cologne playmates spoke German, so Peter Paul grew up knowing at least the rudiments of five contemporary languages.

Posterity has learned of few, if any, incidents and anecdotes that might illustrate the premature budding of his genius. If he showed an early interest in art or displayed an unusual talent for drawing, the world has been deprived of illustrative stories and samples. The biographer considers it mandatory to include such illumination in his account of the early years of a genius, but in the case of Peter Paul Rubens the historian's search is fruitless.

Perhaps the family's continuing problems diverted their attention from a bright child and forced them to concentrate on a succession of crises that appeared unending. Lawsuits in Antwerp threatened the titles of Jan and Maria

Rubens to various properties there, and the harassed wife herself was forced to go off to the city to attend to these matters, leaving her husband in Cologne with the children. Perhaps Peter Paul and Philip sometimes wondered why it was Mama rather than Papa, a lawyer, who looked after business affairs.

In 1580 Claire died while visiting her maternal grandmother, who was herself so ill that Maria had to return to Flanders to take care of her. In 1581, Blandine, now seventeen years of age, became engaged to a Lutheran, and her Catholic parents openly disapproved of the betrothal. Then in September, 1582, Jan Rubens received a shock that numbed him: The legal counselor of Count John of Nassau, one Andreas Christianus, appeared in Cologne and ordered him to deliver himself to the royal authorities at Siegen no later than November 1. Maria's frantic letters to relatives indicate that Christianus hinted the matter concerned the final settlement of the question of the paternity of Anne of Saxony's daughter.

Another term of imprisonment appeared to be looming, and a brief letter Maria Pypelinckx sent to her mother at this time indicates that Jan was contemplating committing suicide. But the problem boiled down to a matter of money. Count John, it appeared, was reluctant to return the 6,000 gold thalers that Jan had posted as bail, and Christianus intimated that Rubens' name would be expunged from the records as the father if he made a gift of the money to Count John.

The poor man, who had already paid for his sins, would have signed anything to be relieved of torment, but his wife had a far stronger backbone and refused. She bargained with Christianus in negotiations that lasted until January, 1583, and in that month both husband and wife signed a document stating that the payment to them of one thousand thalers discharged Count John's debt in full. Jan and Maria had been cheated, to be sure, but had no recourse, although they undoubtedly consoled themselves with the thought that they were free of the House of Orange at long last.

Hendrik died at the age of sixteen, suffering from the same ailment that had carried away Claire. Blandine had second thoughts about her forthcoming marriage and, prompted perhaps by her strong-willed mother, broke off the engagement. Meanwhile political affairs at home occupied the attention of the exiles, too. In 1580 Philip II had regretted the accommodation he had made with William of Orange and, calling the Dutch patriot a traitor, put a price on his head. In 1582 an attempted assassination failed while William was visiting Antwerp, but in 1584, at Delft, a more accurate and daring marksman put a bullet into his head.

The war in the north was renewed, and the fate of Flanders once again was at stake. The Spaniards called on one of their best and most ruthless generals, Alexander Farnese, to restore Philip's full sovereignty to the land, and for a time his cause prospered. But the Dutch and Flemish people rallied to the cause of freedom, the invader was expelled, and Flanders became an integral part of the kingdom of the Netherlands, with the Archduke Albert and the Archduchess Isabella named as co-viceroys for the province.

The way was clear at last for Jan and Maria Rubens to return to their native land with their children, the death of William the Silent having ended the ban against Jan setting foot on Orange soil. The couple immediately applied for passports that would allow them to cross the frontier into Flanders, then settled down to wait while their letter was processed. Jan Rubens did not live to see his native land again.

Worn out by his long struggle against great odds, he died, apparently of a heart attack, one day in February, 1587. His widow and children, including the nine-year-old

Peter Paul, attended private funeral services for him in the Church of St. Peter in Cologne, and he was buried in the graveyard behind the church. The inscription on his gravestone demonstrates the determination of the indomitable Maria Pypelinckx to erase every memory of his disgrace from the consciousness of the world: *"His wife, whom he gave seven children, and with whom he lived twenty-six years in concord without giving her a single cause for complaint, caused this tomb to be erected in honor of her excellent and beloved spouse."*

Late in the year the Flemish authorities granted the family the right to return to Antwerp, and Maria Rubens returned home from exile with her children, including Peter Paul, now ten years old.

The impressionable child must have been disappointed and bewildered by the sights he saw in the city his parents had described to him in such glowing terms. Certainly the reality of the harsh world in which he lived left a lasting scar on the boy and was another factor in the formation of the concepts that became so important in his later work.

Antwerp, once the most prosperous and glittering of the world's great cities, was not dead, as some of her embittered poets cried, but by no stretch of even the most optimistic imagination was she more than feebly alive. Nine long years of destruction and terror had left their marks everywhere. Public buildings were defaced, and approximately forty percent of the private homes in the city had been burned to the ground. Docks, piers, and warehouses had been blown up; proud inns were shells, gutted by the troops that had used them as barracks; and the homes of once-wealthy men were empty, their expensive furnishings and works of art gone. Only the Catholic churches had been left intact, the few Protestant houses of worship, it will be recalled, having been leveled during the "Spanish fury." The population had dropped to a mere three hundred thousand, but refugees and their families who were returning in ever-

32

swelling numbers could find no place to live, and many of them slept in the ruins of their former homes.

Maria Rubens was more fortunate than many who returned. Her funds were almost exhausted, but she was able to obtain food and other necessities from her relatives and those of her late husband who had remained in the city throughout the Spanish occupation and its aftermath. Several of the properties she had inherited were still intact, and she and her children moved into one of these small houses. The weather was cold, and Peter Paul was sent out with Philip to scavenge for firewood, a task that became a daily chore.

In later years visitors to the magnificent home of Peter Paul Rubens sometimes wondered why he kept fires burning in many of the hearths, no matter how hot the weather. He never explained; that he suffered from gout as a mature man may have been the reason.

The people of Antwerp showed a rare unanimity of spirit as they joined in the gargantuan effort to rebuild their city. In the forefront were the Flemish Catholic priests, most of whom had gone into exile themselves rather than tolerate the murder and destruction wrought by the Spaniards. Small boys joined men in the reconstruction work, and apparently Peter Paul Rubens did his part: More than thirty years later, when walking with an English visitor to Antwerp on the waterfront, he pointed to a stone quay and remarked, "I built it with my own hands."

Putting that which was vital to her renewed prosperity ahead of the personal comfort, convenience, and even the need of her people, Antwerp first concentrated on the reconstruction of her port area. New wharves were built, and the authorities made certain they were longer and sturdier than those that had been destroyed. Sunken vessels were raised and removed, obstacles that had been placed in the main channel to prevent the passage of ships were hauled away, and the entire harbor was cleared. Then the Exchange building was rebuilt, and scores of new office buildings appeared; the inns were refurbished and decorated, staffs were hired, and cooks went into the countryside to find farmers who would sell them food on a regular basis. Public buildings were repaired, too, and only after the men and boys of Antwerp had labored unceasingly for a year and a half were the crews of volunteers permitted to turn to the task of building new homes.

By 1589, two years after the return of Maria Rubens and her children, the population of Antwerp had risen to about five hundred thousand, and was still growing so rapidly that the enthusiastic board of aldermen announced their expectation that one million residents would dwell within the rebuilt gates by the end of the century. In spite of their happy pronouncements, however, times were still hard, money was scarce, and trade—the lifeblood of the city— was returning slowly. No one knew the situation better than the widow Rubens, who had moved with her sister, Susanna, and their children into a house the two women owned jointly on the Place de Meir.

Peter Paul and Philip had been taken off the construction crews less than a year after their return and had been sent to the school conducted by Romuldus Verdonck, a scholar and disciplinarian regarded by the older generation as the best of Flemish schoolmasters. Even the sons of nobles who could not afford to hire private tutors sent their sons to Verdonck.

The daily schedule of work at Verdonck's academy was staggering. The thirty boys who constituted the student body left their homes long before daybreak and made their way across the bridges that spanned the canals to the large stone house that, miraculously, had escaped damage during the occupation. After attending mass conducted by a priest whose church was located in the neighborhood, the boys sat

34

down to a breakfast of thick vegetable soup, which contained chunks of meat on days when Mrs. Verdonck could
find beef or lamb in the market. The first class of the day
began while the meal was being eaten and continued without interruption until four o'clock in the afternoon. Latin,
Greek, mathematics, and the classics were mandatory subjects, and the boys were also taught highly colored versions
of Flemish history. Geography was not ignored, because a
knowledge of the world's far places, their products, and
their place in Antwerp's future was important to the sons of
merchants and bankers who were rebuilding their shattered
businesses. Finally, after a supper of smoked herring, bread,
and watered wine, the boys were dismissed, and after walking home in the dark, they sat down to several hours of
composition and other homework.

How Peter Paul Rubens fared under this regimen is unknown, and there is no record of the grades he achieved.
If he felt or showed any artistic inclinations he had no time
to indulge them, since it was Verdonck's theory that a boy
should be kept occupied six days out of seven. On Sundays,
of course, no school was held, but children were not permitted to read or write, and after returning home from church
services, they were sent off to their rooms to meditate on
their sins until they were called to dinner.

One of the more significant outgrowths of Peter Paul
Rubens' attendance at the academy of Romuldus Verdonck
was his first known independent friendship. Balthasar
Moretus was the grandson of Antwerp's most renowned
printer, Christopher Plantin, whose workshop long had attracted the brightest and most gifted of Flemish writers.
Balthasar's father, Jan Moretus, revived the custom of
opening his doors to all authors—this had been his father-
in-law's policy—and the men who gathered daily under his
roof to discuss their world and its future—and to give
Moretus their work to publish—formed one of the most

influential groups in Flanders. It was they, in 1588, who issued the first call to the painters, sculptors, printers, and wood carvers of the Guild of St. Luke to return to their homes; they published pamphlet after pamphlet insisting that Antwerp could achieve greater glory than she had ever known.

It is believed that Peter Paul Rubens was permitted by his mother to visit the Moretus home during school holiday periods, and he may have heard some of the writers' talks since it was a policy of long standing in Antwerp for boys to sit in a far corner of a room and absorb the conversation of their elders. In any event, the friendship of Peter Paul Rubens and Balthasar Moretus grew and deepened, and they remained close for the rest of their lives, long after their paths diverged. Balthasar, who followed the family tradition, eventually became Antwerp's leading printer and publisher. Not only was he one of Peter Paul Rubens' most enthusiastic, loyal supporters, but he is responsible for much that posterity has been able to glean about the enigmatic painter, having collected and preserved most of the two hundred and thirty-five letters Rubens is known to have written.

In 1590 Blandine Rubens made a splendid marriage to a dashing young nobleman, Simon du Parcq, who had inherited an annual income of four hundred florins. A middle-class Fleming at heart in spite of his blue blood, du Parcq was anxious to join several friends in the establishment of a new mercantile company, and for this purpose he badly needed his bride's dowry. But cash in hand was difficult to obtain, and Maria Pypelinckx Rubens faced a new crisis.

She was forced to pay her son-in-law the dowry due him in small sums, and to accomplish even this much she had to practice the most rigid economies. Jan-Baptiste, her eldest son, had just been awarded his master's standing as an apothecary, and since he was starting in business for himself, he was not as yet in a position to help his mother. Philip, who intended to follow in his father's professional footsteps and become a lawyer, had gone off to Louvain, where he supported himself at the university by copying documents for members of the faculty. Eventually he would go on to Italy to obtain his law doctorate and would work part-time as the secretary to a nobleman.

That left Peter Paul, whose education in a private academy his mother could no longer afford. In a move that continues to mystify posterity, Maria Pypelinckx obtained a position for him as a page at the court of the Countess de Lalaing, for many reasons the most unlikely post.

IV

Hendrik, Count de Lalaing, and his wife, Matilda, were both related to the House of Orange, although distantly, and therefore could claim, with some justification, that they had royal standing. In the continuing absence of the Archduke Albert and the Archduchess Isabella, Count de Lalaing was the highest-ranking member of the nobility in the city. Because of his family ties he was entitled to maintain his own court in a palace that had escaped damage during the years of the "Spanish fury," as Madrid had tried to court the favor of his late father.

The new count was a serious-minded man in his early thirties who was devoted to the cause of Antwerp's rebirth. He gave substantial sums to the decimated artisans' guilds, contributed generously to the city's rebuilding program, and quietly became a silent partner in a banking firm that was attempting to reestablish Antwerp as the financial capital of Europe. Like his father before him, he was a patron of the arts and made it a point to buy paintings and sculptures only from local artists.

His countess had less substance and, in a later age, would

have been called frivolous. Independently wealthy and herself able to claim royal descent, she kept her own court in a wing of the Lalaing palace separate from her husband's, and her two small sons, who were being trained for future responsibility by their father, spent little time in her company. She was a vapidly pretty blonde with green eyes, somewhat overweight—as were so many Flemish ladies—and favored the low-cut gowns that became fashionable in the circles of the lighthearted who had grown tired of the austerity imposed on Flanders through so many long years of war.

Why Maria Pypelinckx Rubens elected to petition the countess for a place at court on behalf of her youngest and favorite son is inexplicable even today. It has been suggested that financial necessity gave her no choice, but many other avenues were open to her. It may be that she envisaged a career for Peter Paul as a diplomat, but that explanation cannot be proved.

What makes her decision difficult to understand is that both the count and the countess were related to the late William of Orange and, consequently, were certain to know that the boy who would wear the Lalaing livery was the son of the man who had humiliated the late prince by making a cuckold of him. It cannot be stressed too strongly that Peter Paul, on the eve of his thirteenth birthday, knew nothing of his father's disgrace and punishment. His mother, Jan-Baptiste, Blandine, and the late Claire and Hendrik had banded together to protect him and Philip, and since the family's return to Antwerp other relatives had joined in the conspiracy. Peter Paul knew only that Jan Rubens had been a brilliant attorney who had become Antwerp's principal magistrate, that he had been forced to flee from the Spaniards because of his patriotic leanings, and that his long years in exile had broken his health and spirit.

The boy took great pride in his father, and it can only be

39

presumed that Maria Rubens hoped no one would disillusion him. She was so ambitious for him, as she always had been for all of her children, that perhaps she reasoned the risk of placing him in the service of the countess was worth the possible exposure of the truth. After all, one who became the protégé of a great noble could go far in the world.

Thus Peter Paul Rubens, who presumably was given no voice in the matter, became one of three pages at the court of Matilda de Lalaing, and wore a suit of satin emblazoned with her crest, silk stockings, and shoes with jeweled buckles of gold or silver. Because it pleased the countess to transform her pages into miniature reflections of her own beauty, he was also forced to wear a wig until his own hair grew longer, and the false hair fell below his shoulders in golden waves.

The boy's duties were not arduous. He was required to accompany the countess to church and on all public appearances, and he was in attendance to run errands for her whenever guests were being entertained. He and his fellow pages dined with the family but sat at the foot of the table, far below the salt.

Under the law the three boys were required to attend classes taught by tutors and supervised by the chaplain, and spent no fewer than six hours each day at their studies. The two Lalaing boys also attended these classes, and the count took pity on his wife's pages, who would have enjoyed none of the natural, physical outlets demanded by exuberant youth had he not intervened. As a result of Lalaing's kindness, Peter Paul went out for an hour's canter immediately after mass every morning and learned to ride like a gentleman. He went hunting with the count, learned how to handle a falcon, and spent several hours each week mastering the art of handling a sword. In his later life his impeccable manners, the ease with which he rode and carried his sword, caused most people he met to assume that he himself was a member of the nobility. The fact that his brush earned him an elevation to the peerage of two nations is beside the point and will be discussed in later chapters.

Accustomed to the far more rigorous regimen to which he had been subjected at the academy, Peter Paul had ample free time to do as he pleased. But the palace library was woefully understocked, and he had little to read other than his school books. According to his nephew, Philip Rubens the younger, who wrote his biography in 1576 under the title of *Vita Rubenii,* he discovered the Lalaing art galleries and spent countless hours there, studying and admiring paintings and statues.

Since no student of the life of Rubens can be certain the great painter's nephew was telling the truth, it is impossible to determine whether Rubens' interest in art was sparked and influenced by what he saw in the Lalaing galleries. No other source has ever mentioned the collection as an inspiration to the young page, and Philip Rubens was sometimes inclined to stretch and distort facts according to the dictates of his fancy in order to paint a three-dimensional word portrait of a genius that would explain him to less gifted people. It may be significant that Rubens' first full-scale biographer, Roger de Piles, whose *Abrégé de la vie des peintres,* which was published in 1699, obtained much of his basic material from the work of Philip Rubens, but he took care not to publish any supposed facts he had reason to doubt, and he made no mention of the young page's supposed interest in the works of art that filled the palace gallery.

One of the pastimes of the Countess de Lalaing is known to have made Peter Paul desperately unhappy and, without question, was a factor in the formation of his desire to quit her service. According to a letter that his brother Philip later wrote to their brother-in-law, du Parcq, he was disgusted by the "licentiousness of the court." What caused him to rebel was the role he himself was required to play in the countess' search for pleasure.

When Matilda and her ladies had nothing better to occupy them, it amused her to dress her pages as girls and to force them to maintain the masquerade when she entertained guests. The boys, who were presumably on the threshold of puberty, were stripped of their masculine attire and dressed in the frilliest of undergarments and draped in gowns of rich material. The ladies, who treated them as living dolls, could not resist fondling them. Their eyebrows were plucked, cosmetics were applied to their faces, and long women's wigs were placed on their heads. Then, mincing in their uncomfortable attire, they were obliged to serve refreshments and run errands for the countess' guests, a company that frequently included pleasure-seeking aristocrats who were paying increasingly frequent visits to the reviving Antwerp.

Peter Paul loathed his feminine disguise, although no factual data has ever been uncovered to prove that he was ever compelled to play a female role in sex relations with a man. Certainly the adult Peter Paul Rubens, unlike some of his colleagues, was bluntly and exclusively heterosexual in all of his relationships. But the disguise he was forced to wear in the Lalaing palace shamed him, and one of his fellow pages had already drifted so far into homosexuality that he no longer rode, fenced, or engaged in other masculine activities with the other youths of the court. The boy could turn to no higher authority for protection, and his only recourse was release from his obligation.

According to de Piles and most subsequent biographers, Peter Paul Rubens not only wanted to leave the service of the Countess de Lalaing but was eager to become a painter. De Piles wrote that he had shown no particular aptitude as an artist but "wanted to teach himself to draw for his own pleasure." This factor was only minor, however: "He was

42

spurred, in the main, by his mother's great financial distress, caused by the losses she had incurred during the wars." It is impossible to deny this motive, although he could have gone into some vocation that would have held promise of earlier rewards.

It is astonishing almost beyond credence that for hundreds of years no biographer even mentioned the most significant factor in the character development, personality formation, and career impetus in the life of Peter Paul Rubens. His nephew ignored it, de Piles ignored it, and scores of others followed their example. Like members of his immediate family who tried to protect him by concealing the truth from him, they pretended that the most spectacularly notorious scandal of the age had never taken place.

Rubens himself never mentioned the disgrace of his father to a living soul, yet he learned the whole story. Only one shred of specific evidence to this effect exists, but it is enough. In August, 1591, Blandine wrote a letter to Philip, who had just gone to Italy, and said: "Peter Paul knows the truth about Papa, and is even angrier and more hurt than you were, because you long suspected what the rest of us tried with such diligence to keep from your ears."

Whether the thoughtless Countess de Lalaing blurted out the story to Peter Paul, whether she or members of her court made sly references that enabled him to ferret out the scandal, or whether he pieced together just enough to go to his mother and demand a full explanation is not known and is not important. All that matters is that he knew.

Until he learned the news that may have changed him, Peter Paul Rubens had been a normal, healthy, outgoing boy. He had been devoted to his mother and siblings, had not been averse to the performance of hard physical labor in the reconstruction of the harbor facilities, and had been a diligent student, although he had achieved no academic honors. He had shown no particular vocational leanings and no unusual ambitions but had been content to let the future take care of itself. This may not seem strange in an age when many young men do not find themselves until they have completed their undergraduate studies and have gone out into the world, but in the sixteenth century the sons of the middle class chose their vocations early in life and, more often than not, were entered by their parents as future apprentices of the bankers', merchants', or other guilds before they began their formal schooling.

Above all, Peter Paul had been endowed with a lively sense of humor and enjoyed playing pranks. Balthasar Moretus, who wrote many letters to him over the period of a lifetime, frequently recalled their boyhood escapades and repeatedly referred to Peter Paul's constant laughter.

Now, overnight, everything was changed.

From the time Peter Paul Rubens learned of his father's lurid history his personality and approach to life underwent a profound transformation. An enigma to everyone who knew him, he inspired bewilderment on every level, from reigning monarchs whom he painted and served to the apprentices who labored in his studio, the largest workshop of its kind Europe had ever seen.

He placed an invisible shield between the world and himself and revealed little or nothing of his true nature to anyone except his mother, his sister, and his brothers, a privilege he later extended to his wives, his children, and presumably his mistresses. Even his nephew, in his biography, often referred to Uncle Peter Paul as "austere" and "remote."

As an adolescent and as a man, he never relaxed his guard, never permitted an intimate relationship with anyone outside his immediate family circle. A formal note actually crept into his old friendship with Balthasar Moretus and others he had known since boyhood. His reserve was evident even in times of crisis, and no one ever saw him become flustered or upset, much less lose his temper. Long before he achieved world renown not only as a painter but as one of the most accomplished ambassadors of his day, fellow painters referred to him as "the diplomat" but took care never to speak of him in such terms within his hearing. Rubens severely reprimanded anyone who dared to make a joke at his expense, and a great many of his contemporaries believed that the most serious of his personality defects was the complete lack of a sense of humor.

No one ever saw Rubens laugh, and his portraits, including those he painted himself, show him with dark, serious eyes and a grave expression on his long, sensitive face. If he ever smiled he did so in private, behind the locked doors of his own house, and only in the presence of another Rubens.

He was always alert to the most delicate nuances of conversation, and something in his demeanor made others uncomfortable in his presence; in another, later era he would have been called hyperdefensive. Even kings complained that an inadvertent word or gesture might offend him, and his eldest son, Albert, is the authority for the assertion that he never forgot or forgave an insult. But he took extraordinary precautions to conceal his dislike or even hatred of another from everyone with whom he dealt, including the object of his feelings. Nowhere is this trait more pronounced than in his diplomatic dealings with France, a nation he came to despise. His letters to members of the French royal family and to Cardinal Richelieu, the real ruler of the country, reveal an even-tempered serenity that would make anyone unfamiliar with his inner feelings believe he entertained a judicious admiration for France and everything French.

Anthony Van Dyck, his assistant and later his rival, who remained his friend, once made a cartoon sketch of the master which showed him holding a rigid mask in front of his face. Afraid he might hurt Rubens' feelings, Van Dyck destroyed the sketch, and posterity has learned of it only because other workshop helpers talked and wrote about it.

The self-control Rubens exercised became legendary in his own day. He concealed his real thoughts from all others at all times, revealing nothing either in conversation or correspondence. Those who tried to break down the wall —and there were many—invariably failed, and a man or woman foolish enough to persist was rewarded with a faint lift of his eyebrows which, as any member of the Rubens family could have explained, was a sign of contempt.

In spite of his reserve, or perhaps because of it, Peter Paul Rubens never allowed himself to forget he was a gentleman. He treated everyone, from prince to chimneysweep and chambermaid, with the same impersonal, suave cordiality. A slight nod of his large head indicated he was pleased with the work done by an assistant, whereas a blank expression told an apprentice he had erred. The master never raised his voice, never blamed or praised, and no matter what difficulties he might encounter, never complained.

Soon after the death of his first wife, when many of his relatives and friends—Moretus among them—were afraid he might collapse, he showed no outward sign of grief and is known to have mentioned it in only one letter. In fact, his bland façade caused many to believe, wrongly, that he had not loved his wife for a long time.

Rubens' attitude toward his work demonstrates even more forcibly than does the change in his personality how deeply he may have been affected and influenced by the discovery of his father's scandal and tragedy. From the time the floodtide inundated the young page boy until the day the greatest painter of his age—one of the most extraordinary geniuses in the history of art—lay on his deathbed, his energy, zeal, and devotion to duty were almost beyond the comprehension of ordinary mortals.

At all costs and no matter how great the odds against him, Peter Paul Rubens was determined to achieve so much and to win such lasting renown that the world would forget Jan Rubens' disgrace. No matter how much effort he had to expend, the son intended to force society to revere and honor the name of Rubens for all time, and in this he succeeded beyond his own desires.

His ability to concentrate for long periods to the exclusion of all distractions enabled him to produce a body of work unequaled in any artistic profession, with the possible exception of Honoré de Balzac in the field of literature. In his entire life, from the day he entered his duties as a painter's apprentice until he died, Peter Paul Rubens never took a holiday of any kind. He worked on Sundays, holy days, and other holidays; when traveling overland, he sketched when he paused overnight at an inn; when on a voyage, he set up an easel in his cabin, on deck, or in the main saloon of a ship. He was literally unacquainted with the meaning of rest and relaxation, and he thrived on never-ending work.

In all, he is known to have produced more than three thousand works of art, doing all or the principal portion of each himself, and some authorities believe that the total, including unattributed and lost works, is nearer five thousand. In addition, he was responsible for blocking out countless sketches for the associates in his studio, and for altering, touching up, and filling in innumerable parts and bits of their finished paintings.

Rubens' overwhelming compulsion influenced every facet of his existence. He was known as a generous host and achieved an international reputation for the food and wine he served. Yet on many occasions when he was entertaining, guests who were eating superbly prepared dishes and drinking the finest of vintages observed that he was absently eating bread and cheese, which he consumed with a rough wine or inexpensive ale. He dressed with conservative dignity in attire made for him by the most skilled of tailors, and wore cloth that any prince would have been proud to own. But the *Vita Rubenii* of Philip Rubens the younger indicates that the great painter paid little heed to his appearance, and his assistants frequently were forced to remind him to don a smock in the studio so paint would not smudge his fine clothes.

The same concentration on his work could be seen in both of Rubens' marriages. While still a bachelor, he told Moretus, in a rare burst of confidence, that he would take no one as a wife other than the most intelligent, beautiful, and virtuous girl in Flanders. Both of the young women he married were lovely and honorable, but nothing is known of their intelligence. When away from home, he wrote to them only about mundane matters, telling them virtually nothing about his work, ambitions, or problems. They appear to have existed principally for the purpose of keeping house for him, bearing and rearing his children—and, above all, serving as his models in scores of paintings. He was proud of these ego props and was eager to display and share their sensitive beauty with the world—on canvas.

Universally hailed by his contemporaries as the greatest painter of his age and revered by such geniuses as Van Dyck and Velásquez, their master, Rubens, demonstrated perennial dissatisfaction, demanding that the world unfamiliar with art and indifferent to it nevertheless recognize and honor his name. This inner demand, perhaps enlarged by the fear that somewhere, perhaps, there were people who still might be snickering over the tragicomic exploits of his father, compelled him to seek fame in a realm divorced from art.

It was this unsatiated urge that led him to seek a second career, and his success was so great that not only did he win the recognition he craved throughout Europe, but his services were used by nations other than his own. Sometimes operating in the open, sometimes working secretly, he became an international mediator, and he won the honors heaped on him by grateful kings, princes, and cardinals because of his skill as a diplomat, not because of his talents as a painter.

Only a Peter Paul Rubens who had dedicated his life to the clearing of the family name caused by his father's scandal could have combined and balanced his two careers simultaneously. His ability to juggle them, to use one for the benefit of the other, was amazing. When engaging in a diplomatic mission, he always found time to paint the portraits of the monarchs and great nobles of the country he was visiting. He went everywhere in Western Europe, and he always came home with additional commissions for future paintings as well. When summoned to a foreign court as a painter, he almost always found it possible to obtain simultaneous employment on an important diplomatic mission. In fact, his painting frequently served as a cover for secret missions, and nations from whom he was trying to conceal his missions were none the wiser.

In spite of a double career that brought him immortality, great wealth, renown in his own time, unprecedented honors, and a relatively tranquil personal life, Rubens was an unhappy man. As soon as he completed a painting that even he himself recognized as a masterpiece, his mind leaped to the next, in which he felt compelled to exceed himself. No sooner did he succeed in a difficult diplomatic mission than he sought another, invariably one more difficult. As he made his way to each career plateau, he reached toward one that was higher and, without pause, began his struggle toward it.

His was the ultimate tragedy of the person who demands

for himself the humanly unattainable—perfection—and the dazzling greatness of Peter Paul Rubens' work reflects his recognition of that tragedy while at the same time refusing to accept its inevitability. The sordid scandal of Jan Rubens and Princess Anne of Saxony forged the soul of an incomparable artist.

V When Maria Pypelinckx Rubens learned that her youngest son wanted to give up his life at the Lalaing palace and was willing to sacrifice the benefits he would derive from noble favor, she was badly upset. And when Peter Paul told her he wanted to become an artist, she wept. That, at least, is what Blandine du Parcq wrote to Philip Rubens. She told him, too, that Mama had summoned a family council to discuss the problem; everyone realized that Philip lacked the funds and the time to make the long journey from Italy to Flanders, so Philip's earnest opinion was solicited by mail. Should Peter Paul be allowed to pursue his unexpected goal, or should the request of the fifteen-year-old boy be denied?

Since Philip's letter of reply has not survived the centuries, no one knows what he wrote, but it might be guessed that he approved of the request made by the brother he continued to regard as his closest friend. If so, he was the only member of the family who took Peter Paul's side.

Jan-Baptiste, who remembered not only the flight from Antwerp but his father's scandal and the family's subsequent sufferings, was a man whose insecurity made him a pragmatist in all things. According to a family joke, he counted the gold and silver in his strongbox several times each day, and he was still a bachelor because he was reluctant to assume the expense of supporting a wife. His vote was unequivocal: Peter Paul enjoyed every comfort under the roof of the Lalaing palace and his future was assured if he remained there, but he might become a poor nonentity if he pursued a career as an artist. Du Parcq, who was continuing to badger Maria for the unpaid portion of his wife's dowry, agreed without reservation, and so did Blandine.

Aunt Susanna was a practical person, too, having remained in Antwerp through the years of the "Spanish fury" and the upheavals that followed. Anyone who enjoyed a prospect of obtaining an eventual post in the household of a great nobleman, a position that paid handsome wages, would be insane to think of anything else.

Maria Pypelinckx Rubens cast her vote last, and her voice carried the greatest weight. Although it pained her to deny a request made by her youngest and dearest child, she believed she had no alternative. It would be stupid to leave the protection of the Countess de Lalaing, and thousands of less fortunate boys would be eager to move into the vacated spot.

It must have been difficult for Peter Paul, who never before had defied his mother, to hold his ground. He had no wish to hurt her, but nothing could compel him to return to the service of the countess. Although the mere thought of acting contrary to Mama's wishes brought tears to his eyes, he would act on his own initiative if denied the family blessing.

The boy's firmness created a dilemma that neither Maria Pypelinckx nor any of the others could solve. They needed no reminder of the ancient Flemish and Dutch custom, observed by every guild, that a boy of fifteen was old enough to know his own mind. No longer requiring the approval of a parent or guardian, he could become an apprentice, join a guild, and enjoy its complete protection by signing the necessary application himself. Not even the most antagonistic members of the Rubens' family wanted to become involved in a legal battle with the Guild of St. Luke, which was reviving quickly and was again one of the most prosperous in Flanders. Therefore, a new vote was taken, and the reluctant family unanimously approved of Peter Paul's desire to become a painter.

In order to understand the complexities of the life and career upon which the boy was embarking, it is essential to survey, briefly, the world into which he planned to move. The arts had suffered severely during the decade of war and destruction, when patriotic Flemish nobles and wealthy merchants had lost their fortunes and fled into exile. Now the artists were returning to Antwerp, but their former benefactors were not yet rich enough to buy paintings and statues, sets of leather-bound books, and wood carvings. As a result, the Roman Catholic Church of Flanders became the principal patron of the arts.

A few parish priests protested that their own treasuries were too depleted to bear the expense, but their mutterings were ignored. The bishops knew, if their subordinates did not, that by their pursuit of a deliberate policy of encouraging artists and commissioning their works, the churches of Flanders would become the most beautifully decorated houses of worship in Christendom. Being Flemings themselves, and therefore patriots, the bishops had no intention of confining the work of artists to exclusively religious themes. They commissioned secular paintings and statues that could grace the bishops' castles and priests' rectories, and leather-bound books on secular subjects that would be welcome in the monasteries.

The Italian influences had been strong for decades, and Margaret of Parma had encouraged a freedom of expression that had made Antwerp a magnet for the leading artists of other countries and cities, who had migrated there in large numbers.

Albrecht Dürer, perhaps the most renowned of the outsiders, was a German, a native of Nuremberg who had often visited Antwerp in 1520. Jean Monet, the sculptor, came from Lorraine, and everyone in Antwerp recalled with pride that Jan Provost had come there from Bruges, the city's rival in all things. Lucas van Leyden had deserted Amsterdam for Antwerp, Joachim Patinir had moved from Brussels, and Dirck Vellert was a Frenchman who had taken a Flemish version of his name. There were scores of others, too, and together they were responsible for the creation of a new kind of art, a cosmopolitan one that reflected the Italian influence yet kept its own Flemish character.

Quentin Metsys, the city's most popular painter early in the century, an artist whose reputation has subsequently declined somewhat, is generally credited with being the first to diffuse and soften the harsh religious spirituality of Flemish religious painting. Without robbing it of its strength, he nevertheless endowed it with a grace and charm that previously had been lacking. Metsys was followed by Josse van Cleve and Jan Gossaert, who moved even farther on the road away from stiffness toward a more graceful, easy presentation in which pure colors were predominant.

Gradually the realism of subject matter became less important than style, and the first leading exponent of mannerism was Jan de Beer, who became dean of the Guild of St. Luke in 1515. Thereafter the pendulum moved rapidly, first favoring one school, then the other. Standing somewhat apart from these two mainstreams yet contributing to both was Pieter Bruegel the elder, a supreme individualist of striking power who utilized what he considered the best of every approach and who towered above most of the artists of the period. His nationalistic spirit was evident in most of his work, and this insistently Flemish spirit, which was exhibited in both subject matter and style, gave the Antwerp painters a pride of their own that had been lacking. From the middle of the century they not only felt less dependence upon Italian influences but began to believe, with considerable justification, that they were the inheritors of the Renaissance.

During the lean years of the Spanish occupation and wars, there were virtually no artists practicing their profession in Antwerp. They began to drift back to the city in the late 1570s. Dependent on their only steady customer, the Church, the former refugees and the younger men who began to work with them took no chances, and their paintings, largely confined to religious subjects, reflected a conservatism reminiscent of the primitives done a century earlier. Their work had classical overtones, to be sure, but brilliance of color was lacking, as were all semblances of realism and of the daring spirit that had reached its zenith in the work of the elder Bruegel.

This was the basic situation when Peter Paul Rubens made his entry into the art world of Antwerp. The precise date is unknown, but it is assumed that he began his apprenticeship at some time in 1591, either before or after his fourteenth birthday. His master was Tobias Verhaecht, and although his mother could not have placed him with a less inspired painter, there were few in Antwerp at the time who were better. Verhaecht was a cautious traditionalist who concentrated exclusively on religious themes, and his work ranged from the uninspired to the downright dull. He churned out paintings of such scenes as the Tower of Babel, and these efforts sold for modest sums to parish churches in Flanders that could not afford more grandiose works.

The mediocrity of Peter Paul's master was unimportant at this beginning stage of the boy's career, however, and in no way impeded his progress. He was required to sweep the studio morning and evening, scrub paint splotches from the floors and walls, and perform other menial tasks. Although his early works were mostly on panel, he learned to tack canvases to frames, which he also made. He became familiar with the alchemy of grinding colors, and he not only cleaned brushes but learned how to make them.

It is uncertain how long Peter Paul remained with Verhaecht; according to some sources he remained only a year, while others say it was two years. The precise dates do not matter, and it is sufficient that the apprentice learned the rudiments from a master who had little else to offer him. Peter Paul himself was so conscious of Verhaecht's shortcomings that, in later years, he never mentioned this phase of his apprenticeship.

For all practical purposes his real apprenticeship began at the age of seventeen or eighteen when he moved to the studio of Adam van Noort, a painter with a reputation far superior to that of Verhaecht. He specialized in figure painting rather than landscapes, and it was from him that Peter Paul first began to cope with the mysteries of portraying the human face and figure on canvas.

Van Noort was a man of talent, although most of his contemporaries regarded him as a boor and an ignoramus. He was loud and opinionated, totally lacking in manners or grace, and even those colleagues who were closest to him admitted he was an uncultured lout who displayed no signs of erudition. His table manners were atrocious, and Peter Paul, who ate three meals each day with him, later remarked that even if the food had been better he would have had no appetite.

But van Noort, in spite of his shortcomings, made a significant contribution to the career of the budding artist.

VI On May 8, 1600, almost two years after Peter Paul Rubens received his certificate as a master member of the Guild of St. Luke, the provincial government of Flanders issued him a passport, and the following day he departed for Italy. How had he occupied himself during those two years? He worked for himself in studio space that Venius gave or rented to him, but no details are known.

Obviously he supported himself during that time, and family correspondence indicates that he made regular financial contributions to his mother. It also appears he earned enough to buy a horse and a new wardrobe, and to build up sufficient capital to support himself until he found suitable employment in Italy. These may have been the reasons he waited so long before setting out on his momentous journey.

For centuries nothing was known of his itinerary or the details of his journey, but these gaps were filled by a French scholar and art critic, J. F. Boussard, who published a long monograph on the subject in 1840. Several later authorities have been somewhat skeptical of Boussard's findings, although they have never been able to refute them.

If Boussard is accepted at face value, Rubens was in no hurry to reach Italy. After moving from Cologne to Antwerp at the age of ten, he had not left the boundaries of Flanders, and it was natural that a young man of twenty-three should have been eager to see the world. It is also evident that he had enough money in his purse to afford a leisurely journey. Something even more significant soon becomes apparent. Judging by the prominent people with whom he visited on his travels, he had unexplained connections with the mighty of the world, and this once again raises questions concerning his paternity. Was he the son of Count John of Nassau or of some other prominent nobleman rather than of the disgraced Jan Rubens? The standing of the people who took him into their homes and made him welcome there can be explained in no other way, since his mother and other relatives had no prominent friends abroad and Rubens himself had attained no prominence of his own.

He traveled through Burgundy, and after entering Franche-Comté he spent a week at Arbois as a guest of a wealthy nephew of Mercurin de Gattinara, who had been one of the principal lieutenants of the Emperor Charles V. Going on to Besançon, he paid his respects to Archbishop Ferdinand de Rye, who was the chaplain and confessor of the Archduke Albert and Archduchess Isabella; he spent several days at the archbishop's home.

Still taking his time, he paused at Basle to make a brief but intensive study of the paintings of Holbein, and then crossed the Alps. Most of Flanders lies at sea level, and the mountains had a profound effect on the young visitor, who wrote to his mother that the very sight of them confirmed his faith in God.

Leaving Switzerland and crossing into the Italian states at

the little hamlet of Novalesa, Rubens set out for Padua and Venice. It may be that he chose one or the other of these destinations in order to visit his brother. This would have been natural, but it cannot be proved since Philip's precise whereabouts in Italy at that time were unknown. Apparently Rubens reached Venice at some time in July, and thereafter developments were rapid.

By the end of the month he became a member of the household of Vincenzo I, Duke of Mantua, who, like so many other members of the Gonzaga family before him, was a patron of the arts. Rubens was hired to copy famous paintings for the duke. It was a common practice of the time for a nobleman to hang such copies in his galleries, where they stood side by side with the original works.

How was it possible for a total stranger from a distant land, a young man who had no credentials of his own as a painter, to have acquired a position that was perfect for his needs? Rubens himself offers no explanation. In a letter written many years later, he merely said, "I served the Gonzaga family for many years, and while I was young the delights of a stay in that part of Italy were very much to my liking."

The *Vita Rubenii* tells the story but says little. A nobleman of the Mantuan court, the younger Philip Rubens wrote, met the painter in Venice and took him to Mantua for the purpose of placing him in a position at the court of Vincenzo Gonzaga. This brief tale is a trifle too glib to be accepted without further explanation. Was this meeting in Venice accidental, and was it sheer good luck that enabled Rubens to find the very work he was seeking?

A closer examination of the situation makes the issue even more confusing. Records still extant at the ducal palace in Mantua indicate that Vincenzo Gonzaga visited Venice from July 16 to July 22, 1600, on matters of state business. There is no mention of any meeting or other contact with one Peter Paul Rubens during that visit.

Assuming that the duke and the young artist happened to be in Venice at the same time, how could the unknown have approached the royal personage or a member of his household and obtained a position? One possibility again raises the ghost of Rubens' paternity: If he was the son of a powerful noble, it would have been easy to make the necessary arrangements. The other explanation is also logical: Perhaps Rubens carried letters of introduction from prominent persons in Antwerp or from some of the important men he visited during his journey. However the meeting may have taken place, the young artist from Antwerp was hired.

The duchy of Mantua, located in the Lombardy region of Italy, about seventy-five miles east of Milan, was one of the smaller Italian states and, consequently, was not forced to take part in many of the wars that impoverished the larger duchies. At the beginning of the seventeenth century the population of the city itself was approximately ten thousand, while another five thousand persons lived in the countryside and smaller towns. The little state was far wealthier than its size indicated and was one of the richest states in the Italian peninsula.

There were no industries in the duchy, but the soil was fertile and the farmers thrifty. The city was a major transportation center, and Mantua was one of the few Italian states where extreme poverty was unknown. The Gonzagas, who had ruled the state for three hundred years, were benevolent despots, as clever in making and breaking alliances as they were shrewd in commissioning and buying works of art. As a result of their labors, Mantua had acquired great political and cultural prestige. The duke himself was the overseer of his domain and set broad policies, but day-to-day rule was vested in his secretary of state,

Anabale Chieppio, who had served His Highness' late father in the same capacity.

It could not have been accidental that Rubens soon ingratiated himself with Chieppio, and in spite of the great difference in their ages they became good friends. Surely it was a sign of Rubens' skill as a diplomat that Chieppio called him nephew and granted any favor he asked.

The ancient palace had been constructed in the thirteenth century, but it had been rebuilt and remodeled a number of times. As a consequence, Rubens found himself housed in a suite of his own rather than in the tiny bedchamber under the eaves, to which he had expected to be assigned.

His time was his own; he was free to ask for the loan of paintings belonging to the rulers of other duchies and could copy them at his leisure. Meanwhile the works he saw in the great galleries of the ducal palace dazzled him. Donatello, Pisanello, and Brunelleschi had worked there, as had Mantegna, who had left some of his finest works there. The Gonzagas long had been indefatigable collectors, and Rubens had all the time he needed to study scores of masterpieces by Titian and Raphael, Correggio, Veronese, and Tintoretto. When he wanted to pore over a painting by a great master, he had only to ask for it, and Chieppio sent off a letter to the ducal palace in Florence or Milan. In a rare display of exuberance, Rubens wrote to his mother that he had found heaven on earth.

Daily living was gracious and easy. Vincenzo, who was still a bachelor, dined with the members of his small court, but the painter-in-residence enjoyed the privilege of having his meals sent to his quarters whenever he wanted to eat alone. There were one hundred blooded horses in the stables, and Rubens, who had engaged in no physical exercise since his stay in the Lalaing palace as a boy, went out every morning for a canter. Late in the afternoon, if he suffered from fatigue and wanted to clear his mind, he could wander through the narrow, winding streets of Mantua, where he was recognized by everyone and accorded the respect due an honored member of the duke's household.

Now in full manhood, Rubens had long, dark hair, but his hairline was beginning to recede. He had dark, intense eyes; and, somewhat taller than the Mantuans, he carried himself with a proud air. He was lean, and he walked with a springy, athletic gait that would not change for the rest of his life. The young women of Mantua took notice of this handsome foreigner in their midst, and there are hints in the *Vita Rubenii* that Rubens, with a little leisure at his command for the first time since he had decided to become an artist, returned their interest sufficiently to begin his own investigation of human anatomy.

The artist was given one duty in addition to that of copying great paintings. Vincenzo maintained his own theatrical company, which gave frequent performances for him and the many guests who visited him. It enjoyed the reputation of being the best troupe of actors in Italy. Vincenzo was known as a ladies' man, and the actresses were exceptionally beautiful. When one became the duke's mistress, usually enjoying his favor for several months, the artist-in-residence painted her portrait.

Rubens signed none of these portraits, and since his style was still developing, it has been difficult for experts to distinguish between his work and the thousands of imitations that were purportedly his. But Rubens the man was in a highly privileged position. It had long been the custom of the court, after the duke lost interest in an actress, for his aides to engage in a furious scramble for the girl's favors. The painter from Antwerp was already acquainted with her, having spent many hours alone with her while doing her portrait, and consequently he had first call on an actress whose intimate association with Vincenzo had come to an end. A letter Rubens wrote to Moretus during his sojourn in Mantua indicates that he was neither unaware of the charms of these young women nor unwilling to avail himself of his opportunities. He could not help remarking, however, that the Garden of Eden was not all an outsider might imagine. After a time, he declared, one grew tired of Italian brunettes and redheads and found himself longing for a Flemish blonde. A perfectionist was never satisfied, no matter how pleasant his lot.

There were complications, however, that may have removed the sheen from the Garden of Eden. Another Fleming, Frans Pourbus, was also working at the court of Mantua as a painter. When he returned to the city after a visit to Rome—probably in the spring of 1601—he had seniority. Since he was regarded as the more accomplished portrait painter—certainly he was the more experienced—it must be assumed that he supplanted Rubens as the painter of actresses' portraits, for the next year or two, until the end of his stay in Mantua.

In October, 1600, Rubens accompanied Duke Vincenzo to Florence on an expedition that was to assume great importance in retrospect twenty years later. The head of the House of Gonzaga was betrothed to Eleanora de' Medici, whom he would wed the following year. Consequently, he was given a place of special honor at the most glittering social event of the decade in Italy—the marriage by proxy of Eleanora's sister, Maria, to the great warrior King of France, Henry IV. Henry IV, with his battles behind him, was unifying, modernizing, and strengthening his nation, making her the most powerful on the Continent.

The proxy wedding took place on October 5, and Rubens was presented to the former Florentine princess, now the Queen of France. According to a persistent legend, he chatted with her for a time, and she remembered him twenty years later when she commissioned him to do two series of paintings, one depicting her own life and the other that of

Henry IV, masterpieces that have drawn countless visitors to the Galerie du Luxembourg in Paris.

In the latter part of the nineteenth century a number of art critics created a furor by trying to destroy the legend, claiming that Rubens had not even been in Florence at the time of the proxy wedding, and this claim has persisted down to the present day. But the critics were mistaken, and the romanticists have triumphed; a letter written to Rubens on October 27, 1622, by his good friend Nicolas Peiresc, the distinguished intellectual, dealt specifically with the matter. King Henry had been long dead when Peiresc wrote: "I observed with pleasure that you had been present at the wedding of the Queen Mother at Sta Maria del Fiore, and that you had been inside the banqueting hall."

Presumably the young painter returned to Mantua soon after the celebration. It is not known whether he returned to Florence for the marriage of his employer and Eleanora de' Medici.

Life in Mantua was serene in the winter, spring, and early summer of 1600 and 1601. Aside from an occasional sexual escapade, Rubens buried himself in his work and copied paintings so rapidly that Chieppio was moved to complain. He was being forced too often to write to the rulers of other duchies asking for the privilege of borrowing various masterpieces.

Rubens was demonstrating the thrift practiced by members of his family since the time of their father's disgrace. It is not known what wages Vincenzo Gonzaga paid him, but the duke was not niggardly and, with no living expenses to worry him, it was not difficult for Rubens to send his mother far more than he had pledged. In a letter of thanks, written only eleven months after he had found employment in Mantua, Maria Pypelinckx Rubens wrote him that, thanks to his generosity, she had paid the last of Blandine's dowry and hereafter would be required to spend money on no one but herself.

Rubens remained devoted to her until the end of her days and continued to send her money. Philip also contributed substantial sums to her, although he married soon after his own return to Antwerp, where he became a prominent attorney. It might be noted that Jan-Baptiste did not share his brothers' feelings of loyalty and stopped giving his mother money as soon as Blandine's dowry was paid.

In all probability it was in Mantua that Peter Paul Rubens first fell in love with the work of Titian, perhaps the greatest of the Venetian painters. There were either eleven or twelve Titians in the Gonzaga gallery—various authorities are unable to agree on the precise number—and Rubens copied these paintings for his own instruction.

No man whose work Rubens had yet encountered was Titian's equal as a master of color. According to a story that may be apocryphal, Secretary of State Chieppio came to Rubens' quarters one Sunday after dinner and started to apologize because he thought he had awakened the Fleming from a deep sleep. Rubens' hair was rumpled, and he blinked at his visitor, scarcely recognizing him for a moment or two.

But Rubens recovered and invited the duke's first lieutenant into his quarters to see why he had appeared so distracted. There Chieppio saw "a mound of small canvases," each of them an attempt by Rubens to match the colors—and *only* the colors—in a small portrait by Titian. Another painter might have tried to copy the entire painting, finding the drudgery of reproducing nothing but Titian's colors too exacting. But Rubens, who knew precisely what he wanted to learn from Titian, subjected himself to the harshest of professional disciplines until he learned what he believed he needed. It is no wonder that the colors of Rubens and Titian are so often mentioned together.

In all, Rubens had good reason to be satisfied with his progress as a painter during the first year of his employment in Mantua. He already knew far more than many of his older and more experienced colleagues in Antwerp, but he understood himself sufficiently well to realize he was an instinctive painter. Yet he had to teach himself style, techniques, everything, and the process was painfully slow.

Something essential was missing, and the young painter felt a familiar, creeping restlessness that made him unhappy. He did not yet know it, but he was on the verge of making his most important professional discovery.

VII

Rarely is it possible to isolate a single, dramatic incident in the life of a great man and point to it as the turning point in his career, the key to his entire future. In the case of Peter Paul Rubens, however, there was just such an incident.

In the summer of 1601 Duke Vincenzo busied himself offering financial and other assistance to the Emperor Rudolph, who was preparing to launch a new holy war against the Turks. But the ruler of Mantua still had time to think of his art collection, and on July 18 he wrote a letter to Alessandro Cardinal Montaldo in Rome, commending to his good graces, "Peter Paul, a Fleming, my painter, whom I am sending to you to carry out the copying of certain works of art." The cardinal's reply, dated August 15, confirmed the arrival of Rubens in Rome.

As a matter of fact, Rubens went to Rome to serve two masters. In June the Archduke Albert, regent of Flanders, had written to Vincenzo, asking for a favor. The archduke was titulary dean of the church of Santa Croce in Gerusalemme in Rome, and the interior of the church was in need of decoration. So Albert asked for the loan of the painter to perform the task for him, and Vincenzo, who would have been considered less than gracious had he refused, gave his consent. The triptych that Rubens subsequently painted was his first known independent commission.

Rome, which at that time was still the center of the art world, overwhelmed the young painter. Thanks to the kindness of Cardinal Montaldo, he was permitted to wander where he pleased in the Vatican, inspecting its art treasures, which the public at large never saw. One day he went into the Sistine Chapel, where Michelangelo's superb ceiling, a masterpiece that had required years of hard labor, stunned him. According to his own account, he spent the next week in the Sistine Chapel, absorbing Michelangelo's inspired work.

It was this exposure that was responsible for the setting of his own goal: He wanted to draw with the fire, power, and finesse of Michelangelo, while at the same time utilizing color as Titian had. This dual aim appeared beyond the grasp of almost any painter, but it seems that Rubens did not doubt his own ability to achieve his goal. It might be going too far to suggest that he enjoyed a supreme confidence in his own talents, and it is more likely, in view of the personality that emerged in the correspondence of his mature years, that he believed he could accomplish what he set out to do through Flemish diligence and hard work. At no time in his career did Rubens actively regard himself as a genius, or so his letters indicate. He was a businessman whose profession happened to be that of a painter. Unlike his idol, Michelangelo, who worked with inspired fury, Rubens was always methodical, cool, and disciplined. It was his discipline that was his greatest personal asset, and it, more than any other quality, may have been responsible for his steady progress.

Nothing is known about the paintings he copied for the Duke of Mantua during his sojourn in Rome, but he carried out his duties with such fidelity that he had not completed the triptych for the Archduke Albert by the winter of 1601–2. In January he received an irritated letter from the duke asking when he intended to return to Mantua; in his reply, he begged the indulgence of Vincenzo, asking permission to remain until he finished his work at the church of Santa Croce. It would have caused problems with the Archduke Albert had such a reasonable request been refused, so Rubens was allowed to remain, and stayed in Rome until the late spring of 1602.

The triptych, which is still extant and reposes in the chapel of the Hospice du Petit-Paris in Grasse, is important because it is the first work that can be attributed specifically to Peter Paul Rubens. The centerpiece was "The Finding of the True Cross by St. Helena," which was flanked by "The Raising of the Cross," and "The Crowning with Thorns." These paintings are of interest principally because they reveal how far Rubens still had to travel on his road to greatness. Stiff in both concept and execution, they reveal the Flemish influences of his apprenticeship and are reminiscent of the rigidity that marked the paintings of Venius. But in both technique and spirit, they are deliberately Italian, with the golden tints of the background demonstrating Rubens' indebtedness to Titian, Caravaggio, and the whole Venetian school.

There are hints in the triptych of the gradual ripening of Rubens' genius, to be sure. His emphasis on his central figures reveals his sure grasp of the dramatic, and his technique shows that he painted with great ease. This sure hand, coupled with his intensity of tone, would become Rubens' hallmarks.

Very little can be gleaned about his personal life during his ten-month stay in Rome, but it is possible to piece together some parts of the puzzle from the fragments. It has long been believed that his brother Philip was in Rome at the time, and that the two young men took lodgings together in a house within walking distance of the Vatican. If they followed the custom of the period, they ate their breakfast and supper at the lodging house, and it must be assumed that Rubens' noon meal, which probably consisted of bread, cheese, and wine, was consumed at the church of Santa Croce when he was working on the triptych or in a gallery when he was copying paintings.

Rome was a Mecca for painters, scores of whom were residing and working in the city, and they frequently gathered after dark at small, inexpensive inns near the banks of the Tiber to talk shop, gossip, and drink large quantities of cheap wine. Many of them were unruly and disturbed the peace so often that complaints flooded the Vatican, and Cardinal Montaldo, in an attempt to force them to behave with greater dignity, withdrew the privilege of visiting the Vatican's galleries from the disorderly.

The name of Peter Paul Rubens appears nowhere on the lists of those who were subjected to criticism, and there is no evidence extant that indicates he ever joined these gatherings. He was far too industrious to carouse, and his sober Flemish approach to life would have caused him to avoid the high-spirited painters who slept late after a night of dissipation.

It has been suggested that it was he who painted certain portraits of some of Rome's more attractive street girls, and a few of these works show hints in both style and technique of the artist Rubens would become, but it is impossible to attribute any of these works to him with authority. At the same time, it is difficult to believe that he led a celibate life while in Rome. The actresses at the ducal court in Mantua had introduced him to the joys of association with women, and thereafter the feminine figure never ceased to fascinate him. Unlike some of his Flemish predecessors, who never left the cold of their northern homes, Rubens learned to shed his inhibitions under the warm Italian sun, and at no time thereafter was he a prude. It would be surprising if he had failed to form brief, intimate relationships with some of the attractive young women who came to Rome from farms and villages throughout Italy seeking fortune and adventure. His appreciation of buxom beauty and his knowledge of the feminine figure were too great for him to have ignored the girls of Rome during the better part of the year he lived there.

It is worthy of note that Rubens' vocational and personal activities did not take up all of his time in Rome. His later correspondence reveals that he was very much aware of the world around him during this period. He was absorbed by the power struggle that was waged incessantly by the rulers of Europe, and he followed this tug of war with an interest that would stand him in good stead when he became a diplomat. He also maintained a reading program that demonstrates his interest in cultures other than his own. He may have read the *Decameron* while in Italy, and he gained a familiarity with Machiavelli's *The Prince*. He is also known to have read Benvenuto Cellini's *Autobiography*, which would have been of particular interest to a fellow artist.

Unlike most members of his profession, who dressed carelessly in old clothes, Rubens always looked like a prosperous Flemish merchant or banker when he went out into the world. No one—seeing him walk through the streets of Rome in his well-cut suit of expensive cloth, his hand-sewn boots, broad-brimmed hat, and short-sword—would have guessed he was a member of a fraternity that suffered the disrespect of all honorable, law-abiding Italians. Even the acknowledged geniuses in his profession had never been accepted as equals by the patrons who commissioned and purchased their works, and this was true everywhere in Europe. Rubens was the first to break through the barrier, and his later successes—not only in his native Antwerp, but in London, Paris, and Madrid—can be attributed to his appearance and demeanor. Sober and courteous, with the appearance of a solidly successful businessman, he inspired confidence in the great nobles who treated with him.

His father's disgrace undoubtedly played a major part in this development of his personality, and his reserve, as well as his conservatism, were traits he deliberately assumed. "When I was in Rome," he said many years later, "only the lack of clerical garments made it possible for strangers to distinguish me from members of the clergy."

It is probable that the hard-working Rubens painted more pictures while in Rome than was generally believed for centuries. One work, "The Entombment," which is in the permanent collection of the Borghese Gallery in Rome, long was attributed to Van Dyck, but a number of prominent authorities are now inclined toward the view that it was painted by Rubens. It is similar in many ways to "The True Cross"; and the dramatic composition, the reddish hints in flesh tones, indicate that this obviously Flemish work, painted in a deliberate "Italian" style, may have been done by Rubens.

It is known that Rubens saw something of Scipione Cardinal Borghese, one of the great art patrons of the time, during his Roman sojourn. So it is not going too far to think that the cardinal may have commissioned him to do the painting.

Late in April or early in May, 1602, Peter Paul Rubens finally returned to Mantua, and not only had he received a liberal vocational education, but his purse was heavier. He increased his regular financial contribution to his mother, which indicates that he continued to do independent work in Mantua, but none of the many paintings he may have done there can be authoritatively attributed to him.

He returned to the routines of daily life he had known previously at the ducal court, and for the next year he continued to copy paintings, engage in dalliances with actresses, and take a part in the activities of the court. There was a difference, however: Now he knew what he wanted to achieve, and as he told his assistants and apprentices in his Antwerp studio in later years, "Michelangelo and Titian were never out of my mind."

In the spring of 1603 Rubens' career took a new turn. Not content with the life of a painter as his exclusive vocation, he had started to develop his aspirations as a diplomat, and in some way made these ambitions known to Duke Vincenzo, who approved of his aims and encouraged them by entrusting him with a mission that ordinarily would not have been given to a court painter.

Like all Italian princes, Vincenzo Gonzaga was required to pay homage to the King of Spain, the most prominent and powerful of Catholic monarchs in Europe. This relationship was delicate because the duke, although he could not be regarded as the king's vassal in any technical sense, nevertheless needed the continuing goodwill of the Spanish crown in order to keep his own throne secure.

Vincenzo decided to pay tribute by sending a number of expensive gifts to Madrid, and he needed an ambassador who could make the necessary speeches to express his admiration of the Spanish crown. This post was given to Rubens, who had no previous experience as a diplomat but made a good impression and was, apparently, a forceful and convincing speaker.

Vincenzo's generosity was typical of the man and of the age in which he lived. He sent the king a magnificent carriage of state, complete with a team of six matched horses, as well as a large number of valuable paintings, eleven arquebuses, "six of them in whalebone, and six with rifled bores," as well as an enormous crystal vase filled with rare perfume. Other members of the royal family received quantities of unspecified gifts, and to the Duke of Lerma, the first minister of Spain, Vincenzo sent a large number of paint-

77

ings, some golden vessels, and a large silver flacon filled with perfume. The Countess of Lemos, the king's mistress, was not forgotten, nor was her secretary, Pedro Franqueza, who was said to be the power behind the Spanish throne.

The duke's choice of Peter Paul Rubens as his agent was shrewd. For one thing, the Fleming enjoyed the favor of the Archduke Albert, the uncle of the family-conscious Philip III, a vain young man who left affairs of state in the hands of the Duke of Lerma and other powerful nobles.

Vincenzo's other reasons were enumerated in a letter his secretary sent his permanent ambassador to the court of Spain, Annibale Iberti: "Peter Paul will say what is necessary, like the well-informed man he is. And as this same Peter Paul is an admirable painter, and skilled in portraiture, we desire you, if there are other ladies of quality besides those whose portraits Count Vincenzo obtained for us, to take advantage of his presence and skill."

The ways of royalty were strange, as Rubens quickly discovered. He had been given a mission of considerable importance and delicacy, but the duke hurt his feelings and irritated him by giving him what he deemed insufficient funds to carry out his responsibilities with the style and éclat he believed necessary. The details of his mission are recorded in the reports he sent to Secretary of State Chieppio and are filled with personal asides that tell of his journey in depth, making it unnecessary to resort to conjecture. The twenty-six-year-old Rubens frequently complained of Duke Vincenzo's niggardliness, saying that his lack of funds forced him to adopt an undignified stature not in keeping with his mission. At the same time, however, his reports reflect his extraordinary zeal, and in spite of the handicaps imposed on him, he was determined to succeed.

He personally supervised the wrapping and crating of the paintings, which included sixteen copies by Pietro Facchetti of Raphael originals; and setting out on March 5, 1603, he traveled first to Florence. There, to his surprise, he was summoned to the royal court, where he was received in a private audience by Duke Ferdinand, and his indignant letter to Chieppio still seethes almost four hundred years later:

> I was utterly astonished; I can only suspect that one of my friends has played me false, or that I have been the object of careful scrutiny by observers, not to say spies, living at the court of His Highness of Mantua. The Grand Duke of Tuscany discussed with me in great and knowledge-filled detail my masters, my own vocation and—here is the cause of my surprise—the gifts I am carrying for His Majesty of Spain. There can be no other explanation of his knowledge, because I have given no details of the contents of my luggage, either at the Customs or anywhere else.

Still indignant, he went from Florence to Leghorn, and there found a ship's captain from Hamburg who agreed to take the ten members of the party, the horses and the many packages on board the vessel, and sail for Spain. But the sailor was greedy and, knowing that Rubens served a royal master, charged him accordingly. Again the thrifty Rubens complained to Chieppio.

The voyage was uneventful, but after reaching Alicante Rubens learned that the royal court had moved to a palace in Valladolid, and he started out for that city without delay. The journey quickly became a nightmare that tried the patience of the fledgling diplomat. Torrential rains fell, and the Spanish dirt roads, even then the worst in Europe, became seas of mud. A trip that ordinarily would have taken five days required twenty-six, and Rubens' funds were exhausted by the time he reached Valladolid.

There bad luck continued to hamper him. Ambassador Iberti insisted he had received no message from Mantua regarding the arrival of a special envoy; it may be that his own nose was out of joint because he believed he himself should have been granted the right to present the gifts. He soon relented, however, and not only supplied Rubens with plentiful funds but had a new wardrobe made for him by a Spanish tailor so that Rubens would appear at his best at the court.

Then, inspecting the gifts before presenting them, Rubens made a shocking discovery. Although the canvasses had been protected by sheets of zinc covered by a double thickness of waxed canvas and packed in sealed wooden cases, they had been damaged by the rains which had fallen for more than three weeks, "a thing unheard of in Spain," the annoyed Rubens wrote to Chieppio.

The damage was not irreparable, and Iberti, knowing that the special ambassador was himself a painter, suggested that he repair the Raphael copies. But Rubens displayed unexpected artistic temperament for the first time, and refused, informing Chieppio that "my principles forbid me to mingle my work with anyone else's, however great a man he may be."

He quarreled with Iberti, who referred to Rubens in his own correspondence with great contempt, calling him "a preening flamingo." Eventually, because there was no real choice, Rubens not only repaired the damaged canvases in less than two weeks of feverish work, but painted "several" additional pictures himself, adding them to the pile of gifts. Among them were a contrasting pair, a "Heraclitus" and a "Democrites"; a dispute has raged for hundreds of years regarding the identity of other works presented by Rubens to the king and the Duke of Lerma, and it has been claimed that scores of unsigned paintings were done by Rubens.

At last the great day arrived, and Rubens presented the gifts with great ceremony, making a stirring speech that was well received by Philip III, his first minister, and other members of the court. But the young diplomat's triumph was spoiled by the petty malice of Iberti, who "inadvertently" failed to present him to King Philip and the Duke of Lerma by name, an "oversight" that justifiably annoyed the Fleming.

But it was Rubens who won the ultimate victory. He had restored the water-damaged paintings with such skill that no one, including the king and Lerma, who was supposedly an art expert, realized what he had done. Rubens' account to Chieppio demonstrates not only the vanity he believed he lacked, but also the dry sense of humor supposedly missing in his makeup:

> The paintings, thanks to good retouching, looked very fair, and the accidents they had undergone even gave them the appearance of older works. The Duke took them for originals, for the most part, at least; and he did not, I believe, have the smallest suspicion about them; nor did we, on our part, find it necessary to insist on their authenticity.

Lerma was so impressed by Rubens' own works that he immediately commissioned the painter do his own portrait, an enterprise Rubens initiated without delay. This equestrian figure, done with great verve and dramatic boldness, was confident and spirited and is generally regarded as the first of Rubens' great paintings. Certainly it contained many of the elements that made his later work immortal.

The Duke of Lerma was so pleased with his portrait that he commissioned the young Fleming to do another painting, this one for the Church of the Trinity in Madrid. Rubens went to work with his usual diligence and painted a large triptych: The main panel showed the Holy Trinity, the volet on the left was a portrayal of the baptism of Christ by John the Baptist, and the volet on the right was a representation of the Transfiguration. Playing the double role of painter and diplomat, Rubens managed to include portraits of Duke Vincenzo and his duchess in a crowd scene. In its vigor and warm colors, the triptych was reminiscent of Michelangelo, who was still very much present in the young Fleming's mind.

Rubens was never too busy to continue his own education and studied numerous paintings in Valladolid and Madrid. He wrote to Chieppio that he saw "numbers of splendid Titians and Raphaels . . . whose quantity and quality literally petrified me." That he was becoming increasingly critical in his judgments is shown in a sentence at the end of his account: "As for modern paintings, there is not one worth looking at."

In all, Rubens spent an entire year in Spain, and it is assumed that he painted a number of other portraits during this time, as the nobles were eager to follow the example of the Duke of Lerma. These commissions were not reported to Chieppio, to be sure, since they were the business of no one but the painter, who wanted to make certain his employer did not fail to think that his envoy was devoting all of his time and efforts to the ducal service.

Vincenzo was anxious to have Rubens return to Mantua by way of Paris so that he could pause there long enough to paint the portraits of a number of beautiful women for the ducal gallery. Chieppio went so far as to instruct Carlo Rossi, the Mantuan ambassador in Paris, to rent an appropriate studio for the painter, who was expected to arrive in Paris at any time, having received instructions from Mantua to depart at once. Chieppio also informed the ambassador in Paris that it was the duke's intention to add a new room to his gallery, which would house portraits of the most beautiful women of every nationality.

Peter Paul Rubens did not go to Paris. Demonstrating a new maturity and a boldness that was the direct outgrowth of the success he had enjoyed in Spain, he refused to obey

Vincenzo's order, explaining in a forceful yet diplomatically worded letter to Chieppio that he considered the assignment beneath the dignity of one who was rapidly acquiring a reputation of his own as a painter and who had gained additional stature of his own as a diplomat. The self-confidence Rubens displayed on this occasion never deserted him and remained one of his most pronounced personal characteristics to the end of his days.

Instead of going to Paris, he returned to Mantua, arriving there in the early months of 1604, and discovered that his firm stand had opened a new chapter in his life.

VIII

Vincenzo Gonzaga may have been a man of limited intellect, but he was no fool, and the success Rubens had enjoyed in Spain, combined with his refusal to participate in what he regarded as a cheap enterprise, convinced the duke that the Fleming on his household staff was no mere hack who copied masterpieces but a painter of stature in his own right. So, from the day of Rubens' return to Mantua, he was treated accordingly.

The duke had been told of the triptych Rubens had painted in Spain, and he commissioned another like it. Rubens obliged, working on a larger scale, and this time included not only portraits of the duke and duchess but of other members of their mutual families. The "Transfiguration" is now in the Nancy Museum and the "Baptism of Christ" reposes in the Antwerp Museum. The center section, "The Holy Trinity Worshipped by Vincenzo Gonzaga and His Family," was almost destroyed in 1797 when French troops under the command of Napoleon Bonaparte entered Mantua and, going out of control, sacked the city. The painting was ripped by bayonets, but all sections were

84

preserved, and the main portion is still on display in the ducal palace, while smaller pieces belong to a number of private and public collectors.

The duke was so pleased with Rubens' work that he made the painter a pensioner for life, agreeing to pay him the appreciable sum of four hundred gold ducats per year, payable in quarterly installments. The first payment was made in June, 1604, and Rubens became financially independent.

It was galling to him, immediately thereafter, to receive an order that was lucrative but degrading, and could not be ignored or rejected. Rudolph of Hapsburg, the Holy Roman Emperor, sent a personal letter to the duke, requesting that the Fleming copy two paintings by Correggio that reposed in the ducal palace. Rubens had felt strong enough to defy the Duke of Mantua, but he had not yet achieved enough stature to deny a request from the Emperor. He made copies of the paintings and sent them without delay; they reached Rudolph in late November when he was making his court in Prague. The painter received ten ducats for each painting, a very generous sum, but the money failed to assuage his injured pride.

Immediately after filling this order, Rubens went off to Genoa for a brief visit. Relatively little is known about this sojourn, and it has long been assumed that he went there for the purpose of painting the portrait of the duke's banker. It may be that on this trip he made the acquaintance of a prominent, lovely noblewoman, Brigida Spinola, whose portrait he painted and signed in 1606 on a second trip to Genoa, shortly before the young lady married the Doge Doria of Venice.

The precise length of Rubens' stay in Genoa is unknown, but it is believed that while there he painted a number of portraits wrongly identified a decade and a half later as the work of Van Dyck. Among them were a "Bust of an Old Woman," a "Lady of the Durazzo Family," and "Portrait

of an Old Woman Seated Beside a Young Girl, Standing."
These works are important because Rubens broke with convention, lengthening the profiles of his subjects and adding
rich background detail that added to the nobility of his
work. He appears to have been influenced by the paintings
of El Greco, whom he had studied in Spain.

By November, 1604, when Rubens returned to Mantua,
it was as obvious to the duke as it was to the painter himself
that he had outgrown his employment. He was no longer
a newcomer who could be content to copy the work of
others but a distinguished young painter in his own right,
much in demand. Rubens' desire to leave the Gonzaga
service was made more urgent by the knowledge that his
brother Philip had returned to Rome to obtain his Doctor
of Law degree and was urging Peter Paul to join him.

It was necessary to find a face-saving device that would
enable the duke to retain his pride, and Rubens the diplomat came to the aid of Rubens the painter. He worked out
a simple formula by which Vincenzo granted him his uncon-
ditional release so that he could go to Rome "for purposes
of study." This phrase contained the hint that Rubens
would return to Mantua when he completed his studies, but
in reality this was not his intention. His last apprenticeship
had come to an end, and when he set out for Rome on the
last day of November, 1604, he became his own master, a
standing he would keep for the rest of his life.

Cardinal Borghese, Rubens' friend and patron, had become Pope six months earlier, taking the name of Paul V.
Only fifty-three years of age, he not only had ambitious
plans but was endowed with the power and wealth to carry
them out. The church of St. Peter's was being made the
most magnificent in Christendom, as befitted the cathedral
of the Pope, and the Borghese Palace was being completely
refurbished. The cardinals, many of them members of
princely Italian families, were following the Pope's exam-

ple, and there seemed little doubt that a young painter of growing repute would find many commissions awaiting him. Rubens' struggles were at an end, and his success seemed assured.

No longer forced to count his coppers, he and Philip rented a handsome apartment overlooking the Tiber, a place with a studio, which was essential to Rubens' work. He hired two servants, one a cook and the other a serving maid, and he and Philip ate their meals at home, enjoying the comforts of the gentry that neither had been privileged to know under the roof of their ill-starred parents.

It was possible now for Rubens to take an occasional respite from his grueling, self-induced work schedule, and he took pleasure in the company of various friends. One was Deodate del Monte, a fellow Fleming whom he and Philip had known as boys. Del Monte, also a painter, was a member of a wealthy family and had no need to earn a living, but nevertheless was conscientious. Another friend was Adam Elsheimer, a German painter who did religious and mythological scenes but was mainly interested in the landscapes he was among the first to use as backgrounds. An older artist from Antwerp, Paul Bril, who had spent twenty years in Rome, was yet another member of Rubens' circle. These friendships were important because, for the first time in his life, Rubens established a rapport with colleagues on a basis of mutual respect and could discuss the fine points of professional matters with them.

Thanks to the generosity of Vincenzo Gonzaga, there was no pressing need for Rubens to earn a living, so he indulged himself for more than a year, studying the works of Michelangelo almost to the exclusion of all else. He made uncounted sketches based on Michelangelo's paintings, sometimes working with pen, sometimes in pencil. It is important to note that Rubens was not copying Michelangelo but was learning what he could of human figures, of drama, and of technique from the master he most admired and with whom he felt a sense of kinship. Through absorbing what Michelegelo could teach him, Rubens was expanding and strengthening his artistic talents and concepts.

Sometimes Rubens relaxed after dinner in conversation over a cup of wine with his friends; less frequently, but nevertheless regularly, he availed himself of the services of the ever-present, eager street girls of Rome. But his principal "recreation" was his pursuit of archaeology, in which he had long been interested. He studied the many statues and friezes of antiquity; he prowled through the innumerable ruins of ancient Rome, usually with a sketch pad in his hand; and whenever there was a report of a new archaeological find, which was a commonplace in Rome where coins and statues were unearthed frequently, the Fleming was on hand to view the discovery.

His life was not free of annoyance, to be sure, the principal irritation being the tardiness of Duke Vincenzo in paying the artist's pension. Each quarter Rubens was forced to send dunning letters to Chieppio, communications that were dignified and respectful, yet firm.

It was impossible for Rubens to refrain from giving vent to his own need for artistic expression during this time. "The Apostles," one of a series on the subject, a magnificent painting of heroic figures, which was dramatic in concept and bold in execution, probably dates from this period. So do two mythological works, "Hero and Leander," now the property of the Dresden Gallery, and "Landscape with the Shipwreck of Aeneas," which at one time belonged to Rembrandt, who swore he would not rest until he could equal it. The spirit and freedom that were trademarks of the mature Rubens were evident in these paintings, as were his superb portrayals of the human figure and face. His use of color was totally self-assured, his technique had become his own, and the genius of Peter Paul Rubens was in full flower. Here was no imitator of Michelangelo and Titian but an artist who had learned from both, absorbing what they could teach him, and who now stood completely on his own feet. In 1606, when Rubens was twenty-nine, there could be no question regarding his talents, and Pope Paul V, among others, realized that a major artist had arrived on the scene.

Word of Rubens' increased prowess drifted back to Mantua, and Duke Vincenzo wanted to share in the glory of the man he regarded as his personal discovery. Realizing he could not tempt Rubens to return to the ducal court, which he has outgrown, the cunning head of the house of Gonzaga dreamed up a clever scheme. His Highness, Chieppio wrote, was planning to make an extended journey to Rubens' native Flanders and wanted the artist to accompany him there.

A flat refusal would have been churlish and might have offended some of the cardinals with whom Rubens was enjoying a friendly relationship. But the painter had no intention of being reduced to the status of a quasi-servant again. He was anxious to see his mother, to be sure, but she wrote that she was in the best of health, and he was in no hurry to go home. And like so many young men who dreamed of returning to their native lands in triumph, Rubens wanted to enter Antwerp in triumph, not as the member of a powerful nobleman's suite.

He found a way out of his dilemma. In 1606 he obtained a commission from the fathers of the Oratory to decorate the high altar of a new church, Santa Maria in Vallicella. He had been hard at work on this large project when he heard from Vincenzo, and although his task was almost completed, he went for help to Scipio Cardinal Cafarelli-Borghese, the nephew of Pope Paul and one of the Church's most influential princes. The cardinal, like his uncle a patron of art, was happy to oblige his young friend and wrote to Vincenzo to ask a favor. Would His Highness honor a request from His Eminence and postpone the return of the Fleming to Mantua so he could complete his work on an artistic masterpiece? His Highness, who was trapped, was pleased to honor the request.

There are blanks in the life of Peter Paul Rubens, and one of them occurred in either 1605 or 1606, probably the latter year. He returned to Genoa, where he painted a number of portraits, but virtually nothing is known of the length of his stay. Late in September, 1606, Paolo Agostino Spinola, one of the wealthiest of northern nobles, wrote to Rubens, then in Rome, complaining that the painting the artist had started of him and his wife was not finished. Rubens completed the work and sent it to Genoa.

The visit to Mantua could not be postponed indefinitely without placing Rubens' pension in jeopardy. Since its payment was dependent upon the continuing goodwill of the duke, Rubens must have taken a deep breath early in 1607 as he started off on the familiar road to Mantua. His stay there was brief, uneventful, and boring. He did no known work of consequence and appears to have found some excuse sufficiently compelling to enable him to go back to Genoa.

The architecture of that city's palaces had fascinated him since the time of his first visit there, and he devoted the better part of his stay to making precise architectural drawings, which he published in May, 1622, in Antwerp, under the title *Palazzi di Genova*. The drawings completed, he hurried back to Rome and made a tactical error by not pausing in Mantua. Vincenzo, immediately aware of the slight, withheld payment of Rubens' pension and sent him a brief letter, virtually commanding him to come back to Mantua.

Rubens' reply, written a few months before his thirtieth birthday, illuminates the character of a man who had

reached maturity. He was self-assured without being arrogant and was conscious of his honor and dignity; at the same
time he was a clever diplomat who would not knowingly
offend someone who was valuable to him and who could
harm him if he overstepped the mark. Ever mindful of the
scandal that had ruined his father, he walked an invisible
tightrope in his relations with the mighty, while at the same
time remaining aware of his own reputation, talent, and
growing stature. He wrote:

> I do not know to whom to apply in order to obtain
> the favor I seek, if not to Your Highness, thanks to
> whom I have already received one of the same kind.
> I refer to the four months' honorarium so promptly
> paid me by Your Highness. Time has passed quickly,
> and I am again owed for four months.
>
> I am vexed by His Most Serene Highness's decision
> which commands me to return to Mantua at such short
> notice that it cannot be obeyed. I cannot, as a matter
> of fact, think of leaving Rome at such short notice,
> owing to some considerable works which I freely con-
> fess to you I was forced to undertake after a whole
> summer of application to my art, because I could not
> honorably maintain a house and two servants in Rome
> with only the 140 crowns which are all that I have
> received from Mantua during my absence. Besides
> which, this is the most happy opportunity imaginable
> of taking advantage of my skill and thirst for work.
>
> It is the ornamenting of the high altar of the new
> church of the Oratorian Fathers, Sta Maria in Valli-
> cella, the most renowned and fashionable of all
> churches in Rome.
>
> The letter of credit for fifty crowns, payable on sight,
> is to hand. The lateness of its arrival—by a mere few
> days—is of small importance, since it has in no wise

incommoded me; indeed, Your Highness shows too much kindness in thus honoring his servant with confidences and excuses in respect of such trifling matters.

Rubens' first self-portrait, painted in Rome at about this same time, confirms the impression of his personality conveyed by his letter. He was handsome and well dressed, somewhat taller than most of his contemporaries, and his bearing was that of a man who was conscious of what he had achieved and believed he would travel much farther on the road to success. He was solidly built, the girth of his legs and upper arms indicating he might be a trifle overweight, which is not surprising. Like all Flemings, he appreciated food and drink, and although he paid no attention to his meals when he was concentrating on his work, he had learned to relax over a leisurely meal when he had completed his day's efforts. Only in his later years, when his reputation reached its zenith, did he become so absorbed in his painting and in the pursuit of his secondary career as a diplomat that he lost all interest in what he ate or drank.

There is some reason to believe that during this stage of his life in Rome the thirty-year-old Rubens became involved in his first serious romance. All that is known, however, is based on a fleeting reference made by Philip Rubens in a letter to Blandine du Parcq, and an even more obscure hint in the biography written by Philip the younger. Apparently the young lady was a member of the Roman aristocracy, and for a time, at least, she reciprocated Peter Paul Rubens' affections. It is impossible to determine what ended the romance, and it can only be guessed that the proud parents of an attractive young Roman patrician would have objected strongly to her marriage to a foreigner from the north, particularly a mere artist who could claim no standing for himself as a member of the nobility.

Rubens himself made no mention of the young lady in his

letters to his mother or anyone else. Exceptionally sensitive in such matters because of his father's troubles, he maintained a lifelong, habitual silence on the subject of his private life, which he kept separate from his career. Some of his nineteenth-century biographers speculated that the girl was a member of the Borghese family, but there is no basis in fact for any such assumption, and it is probable they were indulging in daydreams. A member of one of the wealthiest and most powerful princely houses in all Italy might have been attracted to Rubens, of course. But he would have been far too cautious to allow himself to engage in intimate relations with any woman who was a member of a social class so far above his own. His father's catastrophe had not stemmed from his adultery as such but from the fact that his mistress was a princess, and it is inconceivable that Peter Paul Rubens, who never completely overcame his feeling of shame, would have made the same terrible mistake.

IX In 1607, his last year in Rome, Peter Paul Rubens came into his own. He moved freely in the highest circles, as did Philip, who had become the librarian-secretary of Ascanio Cardinal Colonna, a nephew of the head of a princely house that rivaled the Borgheses in power and wealth. The Rubens brothers established something of a salon, but it was unlike many others in the city because of its sobriety. Most of the men who dropped in at the Rubens' house for an evening were archaeologists, both brothers having made a study of the ancients their avocational passion.

Peter Paul made many sketches of ancient statues, coins, and ornamentation, and it is posterity's misfortune that most of these drawings were lost in a fire a short time before his departure from Rome. A number of them appeared in a book for which Philip supplied the text. It was published in Antwerp in 1608 by their childhood friend, Moretus, under the title *Electorum Libri Duo,* and the engravings of the drawings were made by yet another friend in Antwerp, Corneille Galle.

Rubens' dedication to his work was already almost legendary, and when his friend, Elsheimer, died of an unknown illness that carried him away before he reached the prime of life, Rubens wrote to a German physician, Johann Faber, that he was certain Elsheimer had been killed by "the sin of sloth."

Nothing in the worlds of art and politics, no matter how seemingly insignificant, failed to interest the painter whose work was giving him an international reputation. Rome was shocked by the harshly realistic paintings of Caravaggio, whose work was shunned by respectable patrons and artists alike. But Rubens braved the possible scorn of men whose friendship was valuable to him and spent several weeks making an intense study of Caravaggio's paintings.

It is believed that the two artists had become acquainted in Rome, although nothing specific is known about the relationship they may have enjoyed. Certainly Rubens saw his colleague's great works in San Luigi dei Francesci in Rome. By 1607, when Caravaggio's work was beginning to revolutionize Italian art because of his stark concepts of light and color, the Lombard himself was no longer in the city. He had killed a man in a duel the previous year, and after fleeing to the Sabine hills, he was alleged to have found refuge in Naples.

There was no real need for Rubens to hold any discussions with his fellow painter at this juncture, however, because Caravaggio's paintings spoke for themselves. The emotional tensions that were ever-present in the Lombard's work, combined with his insistence on clarity, had an effect on Rubens that would manifest itself in years to come, just as it influenced every other major artist of the period and of later eras.

By this time Rubens had evolved his own style and approach, but his elasticity was remarkable. Neither then nor later did he feel he was too old to learn, and even when he became the most famous artist of his age, commanding fees far larger than any other living painter could ask, he continued to utilize ideas, approaches, and techniques of colleagues when these appealed to him and gave him reason to believe that their adoption would enhance his own work.

Perhaps the greatest contrast to be found in the life and the work of Peter Paul Rubens is the difference between his private and vocational existences. As an artist, he was a liberal always eager to learn, experiment, and adopt anything that could be of help to him and improve his paintings. In his thinking, he was a devoted humanist who studied the art and culture of the ancients with a zealous passion and who, through that study, became a devoted disciple of the principles of individual human dignity. At the same time, however, he was essentially conservative at all times in his private life, which he went to great pains to keep private.

When others drank to excess in his company, he made a point of sipping heavily watered wine, and he left any company that became boisterous. When he associated with a Roman street girl their relationship was a closely guarded secret, and perhaps even Philip did not know the identity of the young women his brother sometimes entertained in their home. The conservatism of Rubens was manifest in his manners, his dress, even his speech, which was inclined to be ponderous—if the letters of a number of people who came in contact with him through the years can be trusted. His colleagues were contemptuous of convention and often were deliberately iconoclastic in breaking the social rules of society. But Peter Paul Rubens comported himself with the dignity of a Flemish banker.

Perhaps the most impressive fact to be gleaned in a perusal of Rubens' life in 1607 was the extent of his activities. He was engaged in two major projects, either of which would have occupied almost any other artist to the exclusion of all else, but he found—or made—the time for much that interested him. When a member of the Gonzaga family became a cardinal, the artist made an intensive study of the Palazzo Capo di Ferro in Rome, which Duke Vincenzo wanted to buy for his relative, and sent him a long report, complete with many sketches, on the architecture and on the contents of the art gallery in the palace. Rubens is also known to have attended many meetings of a learned society devoted to a study of archaeology, and on several occasions in 1607 he addressed the group, having become sufficiently expert to be considered an authority in his own right.

Then catastrophe struck. He completed his altarpiece for the fathers of the Oratory, "Adoration of the Virgin by Angels and Saints," which excited all who saw it and won praise from everyone. But he discovered that the painting could not be mounted because the light that filtered in through the windows of the church obscured it in shadows, and he wrote a disturbed letter to Chieppio: "One can hardly distinguish the figures, or enjoy the perfection of the colors, the style of the faces and the folds of the draperies, though they have been treated with extreme care, and are done from nature—and are agreed by everyone to be beautiful!"

In order to fulfill his contractual obligation Rubens found it necessary to paint the picture a second time, doing it on a porous slate that absorbed the oil in his paints and gave the completed work a dull finish. The second version, which is still on display in Sta Maria in Vallicella, is considered by many authorities to be distinctly inferior to the first, now owned by the Grenoble Museum. Not surprisingly, the work done on slate is said to lack the spontaneity and warmth of the original, although both—conceived on a grand scale, with figures that seem to come alive—are regarded as masterpieces.

The "Adoration of the Virgin" confirmed Rubens' reputation as an artist of the first rank, and not only was he inundated with offers of new commissions, but Duke Vincenzo redoubled his efforts to persuade his once-personal painter to return to Mantua, even hinting, in letters actually written by Chieppio, that he might be compelled to cancel Rubens' pension unless the Fleming complied with his wishes.

But Rubens was in a position to ignore the threat, although he never gave up any money if he had a choice in the matter. According to a story that may be apocryphal, an incident that took place in Antwerp a few years later illuminates the point. According to this legend, a very wealthy French noble came to Antwerp for the express purpose of having his portrait painted by Rubens, and when the task was done, the noble expressed shock at the price he was being charged, claiming he could not afford to pay it.

"How much *are* you willing to pay?" Rubens is supposed to have asked.

The nobleman named a paltry sum that was approximately one-third of the asking price.

Rubens agreed without hesitation, then picked up a brush and with a single stroke obliterated his signature from a corner of the painting.

The nobleman, reacting just as quickly, changed his mind and agreed to pay the full asking price, whereupon Rubens wrote his signature in another corner of the work.

The Orations believed they had first call on Rubens' services, and he agreed with them, his loyalty to patient friends weighing more than the considerably larger offers he received from other sources. So he accepted a commission to paint the decoration for the high altar at the church of S. Filippo Neri at Fermo, and went to work without delay. The "Adoration of the Shepherds," although conceived on the same heroic scale as his previous work, must be regarded as one of his more disappointing efforts. The pure, bright colors that were usually in evidence in a painting by Rubens were drowned in a sea of dull browns that created a tepid, uninspired effect. In fact, the "Adoration of the Shepherds" is so unlike most of Rubens' paintings that it was "lost" for centuries, even though it remained in the church in Fermo, and not until modern times have a number of authorities established the work as his.

Rubens' first painting of the "Adoration of the Virgin" was still on his hands, which annoyed him, and the fact that the second was being seen daily by Romans made it impossible for him to find a buyer in the city. After due contemplation the thrifty Fleming thought of selling it to Vincenzo of Mantua and wrote to Chieppio that "it would not be to my honor to leave in Rome two similar paintings from my hand."

Knowing that the bargaining would be furious and prolonged, he set an outrageously high price for the painting, and as he had anticipated, the duke rejected it. Rubens wrote to Chieppio again, graciously suggesting that Vincenzo pay any sum he considered fair. But he could not forget that His Highness of Mantua hated to part with money, regardless of whether he had made a firm agreement. So Rubens was moved to add a postscript saying he needed a minimum of one to two hundred crowns on account in order to incorporate into the painting features that appeared only in the second.

Vincenzo could remember the day in the not-too-distant past when the sum of one hundred crowns had purchased Rubens' services for an entire year. So it is not surprising that the duke procrastinated, perhaps hoping to obtain an even greater reduction in price.

Rubens refused to take the bait, and his approach became casual. The painting had been on exhibition for several days in the church for which it had originally been intended, he wrote, apparently neither knowing nor caring that the duke, with a slight effort, could learn that it had actually been stored in the church cellar, and that its wrappings had not been removed. It had been seen under appropriate lighting, he declared, and had been so admired that he felt certain he would find a buyer "within a few days" who would meet his original price.

When Vincenzo Gonzaga was threatened financially he could be the most miserly prince in Italy, and he sent off a letter to Rubens in his own hand, informing the artist that he had no intention of purchasing the picture and wishing him good fortune in finding another buyer. His intimation was that it would not be easy to find someone else who would buy the painting.

The deliberate insult infuriated Rubens. In fact, his anger was so great that he dropped his mask of polite caution, and his reply allows posterity to see the egocentricity of the artist who was usually hidden behind the façade of a businessman and diplomat. His Highness, he wrote, had been giving so many festivals that it was not surprising he lacked the money to buy a superb painting, and his attitude was scarcely surprising to one who knew that even the treasuries of princes far wealthier than the ruler of Mantua were not unlimited. Then, displaying unprecedented arrogance worthy of a king, he added: "The treasury of Mantua would scarcely have been in any hurry to give me financial satisfaction; it is certainly in no hurry to pay me the salary I have been owed for a long time.

"For that reason I finally begin to consider the failure of my proposition as a stroke of good fortune."

That letter, sent in the early summer of 1607, was the last that Rubens ever wrote to the head of the House of Gonzaga. Apparently he realized he would receive no additional pension payments, and he ended the relationship by expressing his true opinion of his former employer and patron.

The duke believed he would have the last word. He was

finally preparing to embark on his delayed journey to Antwerp and Brussels, and he sent a cold order to Rubens, commanding him to present himself in Mantua within two weeks, ready to begin the journey.

Rubens elected to ignore the summons, which no court outside Mantua would uphold and, having burned his bridges behind him, did not deign to reply.

Philip Rubens obtained his law degree sometime during the summer of 1607 and departed at once for Flanders, leaving his younger brother alone in Rome. In September he sent Peter Paul a letter filled with catastrophic news: Blandine was dead, and Maria Pypelinckx Rubens, now seventy-two years of age, was suffering from a severe attack of asthma and was not expected to live.

Rubens immediately concluded all of his remaining business in Rome, and within seventy-two hours of his receipt of his brother's letter he, too, was traveling to Antwerp. Changing horses frequently, he rode each day until he was exhausted; when possible, he snatched a few hours of sleep at an inn, taking bread and cheese to eat on the road, but often he paused in a patch of woods and rolled up in his cloak to await the first light of dawn that would enable him to resume his journey.

Rubens' dream of entering Antwerp in triumph was forgotten; no one knew he was coming, and no welcoming committee was on hand to greet him when he presented his passport at the city gates late one day in November. In fact, it is unlikely that even old friends would have recognized the gaunt, travel-stained man.

Philip Rubens was alone in the family dwelling that Peter Paul remembered so vividly and greeted him with the news that their mother had died a month earlier. In accordance with her own wish she was buried in the Abbey of St. Michael near the city, and Philip said that in her last breath she murmured the name of her late husband.

Philip the younger reveals in the *Vita Rubenii* that the painter visited his mother's grave alone, and when he returned home, his face tear-stained, he retired behind the closed door of his boyhood bedroom and did not emerge for forty-eight hours.

Soon thereafter the few living members of the Rubens family attended a memorial service at the tomb of Maria Pypelinckx. She was survived by only three of her children, Jan-Baptiste, Philip, and Peter Paul; the next generation was represented by Blandine's son and two daughters, and by Jan-Baptiste's two sons. Balthasar Moretus is the authority, in his correspondence, for the assertion that Rubens announced his intention of designing a memorial to be erected over his mother's grave, but that he so lacked heart for the enterprise that he never finished it, even though he made many sketches and designs.

The shock of Maria Pypelinckx's death immobilized Rubens, and almost nothing is known of his activities for about two months after his return to Antwerp. He spent most of his time at home, refused to see old friends, and grieved in private, unwilling or unable to permit others to see how much he was suffering.

Philip, who was following in his father's vocational footsteps, had already become one of the most prominent and influential citizens of Antwerp, even though he himself had only returned home a few months earlier. He had been appointed to a post as one of the four "municipal secretaries" of the city, but his duties as a member of this board of ruling aldermen in no way interfered with his private practice of law, which was already flourishing. He had also met the twenty-three-year-old daughter of Henri le Moy, the head of the council of municipal secretaries, and had become engaged to marry her. His own future appeared secure, and he asked Peter Paul to remain in Antwerp for his wedding, which would not take place until the following spring after a six months' period of mourning for his mother.

The hasty trip of Peter Paul Rubens had carried him from the warmth of Italy to the cold climate of northern Europe, and according to contemporary accounts the winter of 1607–8 was one of the most severe in many years. Rubens missed Rome, the center of the art world, but a sense of obligation to his brother made it necessary for him to remain in Antwerp for several months, and he had made no long-range plans. As 1607 came to an end he had no idea whether he would return to Italy or remain in Flanders. All he realized for certain was that he would receive no further pension payments from Vincenzo Gonzaga, and even though he had come home with a full purse, it would be necessary for him to earn a living.

X By the latter part of the seventeenth century's first decade the Low Countries were enjoying unprecedented quiet in an atmosphere of extraordinary security. Western Europe was at peace, and nowhere else did the prospects for its continuance seem more promising. The Netherlands was flourishing as an independent nation, and Flanders, associated with it while remaining under nominal Spanish rule, was no longer a bone of contention. The Archduke Albert and Archduchess Isabella, who were on the verge of moving their capital from Brussels to Antwerp, enjoyed the strongest of ties with both the House of Hapsburg and the House of Orange, being related to both. Albert was the uncle of Philip III of Spain, but the most prominent member of his court was the Count von Buren, a son of William the Silent, the martyred patriot who had been murdered at the instigation of Philip II. Also present was Count Louis of Egmont, whose father had been beheaded by the Duke of Alba during the worst days of the "Spanish fury."

Thanks to the efforts exerted by a compassionate Albert and a gentle Isabella, Flanders enjoyed an aura of tolerance almost unknown in other parts of Europe, where religious strife was creating civil wars and reigns of terror. Catholicism was the faith of the majority in Flanders, and the Church was active in every phase of public life, but Protestants were not molested and lived without fear. Even the Jews, long harried in so many lands, were permitted to worship as they wished and were no longer confined in the ghettos that had been the shame of Western Europe during the harsh age of Philip II.

As a result of Albert's persistence, the Spanish garrisons that had occupied many of the towns in Flanders had been withdrawn, and the laws that had restricted Antwerp's trade, although never repealed, were universally ignored. The city was recovering from her long years of depression, and new industries had come into being: She made glass, textiles, and tapestries; she had become the largest paint manufacturing center in Europe; and her craftsmen were respected everywhere.

Albert was not strong enough to rule in his own right, and he knew it. Thanks to his independent spirit he received no financial assistance from Madrid, but the people of Flanders were glad to pay a high price for their liberty and submitted cheerfully to heavy taxation. A Genoese soldier, Ambrogio Spinola, was the commander-in-chief of the armies of the Low Countries, and local youths flocked to his banner, enlisting happily as they took the places of the Spanish troops who had departed. A quarrel with Holland kept the Scheldt River closed to trade, which injured Antwerp's economy, but the people were optimistic, and the difficulty was resolved a little more than a year later.

A new era of prosperity appeared to be at hand, and Peter Paul Rubens must have been aware of it as he assessed his future. A return to Rome would make it inevitable that he would quarrel again with Vincenzo of Mantua, a prince who lacked real power on a broad European scale. If he remained in Antwerp, however, he knew he would enjoy the active protection of Albert and Isabella, who had long admired his work. He was acquainted with the Marquis de Spinola, thanks to the portraits he painted of the general's relatives in Genoa, and his own former master, Otto von Veen, was the official painter at the court of the regents and also held office as director of the mint. In addition, Philip Rubens was a man of consequence in Antwerp now and was in a position to be of great help to a brother who would have to work hard to establish himself in the art world if he decided to remain at home.

If Rubens expected a royal welcome from his fellow citizens he was doomed to disappointment. The artists of Flanders made up a closely knit group, and he had been away for a long time, sufficiently long to be half-forgotten. It is true that he had acquired an international reputation by painting some very large church canvases while in Italy, and it was also true that he had made something of a name for himself during the year he had spent in Spain. But Antwerp preferred painters who reflected their own intensely nationalistic traits to those who were followers of the more sophisticated Italian school.

When Rubens emerged from his period of deep mourning for his mother, he learned from Moretus and other old friends that, if he decided to remain in Antwerp and practice his profession there, the city would confront him with a "show me" attitude.

Rubens knew himself: His ambitions were boundless, and he himself realized, even if the rest of the world had not yet become aware of it, that he could and would become the greatest painter of his time. This judgment was not based on mere vanity but was a sober appraisal of his own talent and potential, as opposed to that of the other young painters whose work he had seen and studied. He recognized in himself an almost unlimited capacity for work, and it has been said that he knew he sublimated the ultrasensuality of his own inner nature in hard labor. His self-control was absolute, ruling him in all things, and he never called undue attention to himself in a crowd. Even in his approach to religion he was moderately pious, attending mass every Sunday but otherwise paying little attention to the questions of theology that other men found all-consuming. This made it all the more remarkable that he numbered so many high-ranking clergymen as his patrons and friends.

It is of the utmost significance that, when he built his own home in later years, he had two quotations from Juvenal carved in stone over the entrance to his garden. These constituted his rule of life, he said, and he tried to live accordingly:

> Let us leave to the gods the care of dispensing their benefits to us and of giving us what we most need. They love men better than men love themselves.
> Let us ask them only for health of body and soundness of mind, for a strong soul free from the fear of death and untouched by anger or by vain desires.

In the light of Rubens' character, fully formed by the time he came back to Antwerp, it appears inevitable that he elected to meet the challenge of his own people and country and remain in Flanders rather than return to Italy. The people of Antwerp shared his sober approach to life, and he truly felt more at home there than he had in a land where few men worked hard and frivolity was not regarded as disgraceful. The man who would become the art world's leading exponent of the Counter-Reformation was endowed with an overpowering intellect, but his religious beliefs were simple. He had faith in God, he accepted the Trinity, and it did not occur to him to rebel against the One True Church. His own tolerance made it possible for him to become the good friend of men of many faiths, and his attitude was reflected in the spirit shown by the Church in Flanders. Certainly he could not have remained content for years in Spain, where Protestants and Jews were not permitted to worship.

Rubens' decision to remain in Antwerp was not made overnight but was a gradual process. He knew he would stay for a few months, until his brother's wedding, and his visit was prolonged when the illness of Philip's future father-in-law forced the postponement of the marriage for several months. In the meantime Peter Paul needed a place to work; he made a studio for himself on the top floor of the house that had belonged to his mother and, in the late spring of 1608, even installed a skylight of his own design that would enable him to gain the full benefit of the weak Flemish sunshine.

It is probable that the intervention of two powerful men confirmed his decision to stay in Antwerp and resume his career there. The Archduke Albert sent for him, and when Rubens reached Brussels he was overwhelmed by the regent's offer: He could name his own fee for a portrait of the archduke and archduchess, and Albert also hoped he would consider the acceptance of other assignments. Rubens returned to Antwerp after promising to think about the matter.

He no sooner reached his home than he received yet another offer, this one from the most prominent citizen of Antwerp, Nicholas Rockox, who held Jan Rubens' one-time post of chief magistrate and who had served for a number of years as mayor of the city. Certainly it is not lacking in significance that the offer came to Rubens from a man who had been a friend and associate of his father, who undoubtedly knew the sordid story of the elder Rubens but was willing to overlook it in order to offer important work to his son.

Rockox asked Rubens to paint an "Adoration of the

Magi" for the chamber of state in the Antwerp Town Hall, a room already filled with precious works of art. Unable to resist—and his own inner decision already having been made—Rubens accepted the offer. A second commission of equally great importance came to him two years later from Rockox and resulted in one of his supreme masterpieces, the "Descent from the Cross," which was to appear in the chapel of the Serment des Arquesbusiers in Antwerp's Cathedral of Notre Dame.

In the summer of 1609 Rubens returned to Brussels at the request of the archduke. Venius having been given another post in order to move him out of the way, Rubens, who had been born in exile, was given the official appointment of "painter to the palace of their Serene Highnesses" at an annual salary of five hundred gold francs. Not only was the appointment a flattering guarantee that Rubens would enjoy the protection of Albert and Isabella, but his salary was double the pension he had been paid, sporadically, by Vincenzo Gonzaga.

Ordinarily a painter holding such a post would have been required to live at the court of his patrons, but Albert and Isabella, in spite of their repeated promises to move to Antwerp, continued to linger in Brussels, where the royal palace was more to their liking than any home they might have found in the bustling port city. On this occasion Rubens displayed a shrewd, tough approach that made it possible for him to pursue his career.

Life at court was pleasantly sybaritic, but he had enjoyed his fill of royal courts and knew he could not do his best work in a place where constant interruptions would occur because his presence would be required at various social functions and affairs of state. Showing a rare courage, he informed the archduke he would accept on condition that he could make his home in Antwerp. How Albert reacted to this unique request is unknown, but he had long recognized Rubens' extraordinary talent. (It will be remembered that the painter had done a canvas for him several years earlier for the Church of Santa Croce in Rome.) Albert accepted the condition and the appointment was made.

On October 3, 1609, Peter Paul Rubens was married to Isabella Brandt, a native of Antwerp, at the church of St. Michael. Virtually nothing is known of the romance of Rubens and the lovely, dark-haired Isabella other than that they probably were introduced to each other by Philip's wife, who was Isabella's close friend and contemporary.

The bride was the daughter of the clerk of the court of Antwerp, a man who had held this post for a short time before Jan Rubens had been forced to flee into exile. This fact cannot fail to have importance: A father who knew of the scandal attached to the name of the elder Rubens nevertheless allowed his daughter to marry a son of the disgraced magistrate!

Brandt was a humanist, sharing Rubens' interest in classical antiquity, but nothing is known of interests that the bridegroom shared with his bride. Rubens was thirty-two years of age when he married, and Isabella, fourteen years his junior, had just passed her eighteenth birthday. She had received some education at a convent school in Antwerp but, in the main, had been educated at home, as was usual with the daughters of the middle class.

She was pious, and under her influence Rubens attended mass daily instead of going to church only on Sundays, but in other respects it was the husband rather than the young wife who was the predominating influence in the home. For the first years of his marriage, until Rubens could afford greater elegance, he and Isabella lived in his mother's old house, and his work habits, his way of life, remained unchanged.

Isabella's personality and appearance are best described by Rubens himself in a husband-and-wife portrait he painted soon after their marriage. She was tall, with dark hair and eyes, long and aristocratic hands, and only the roundness of her face hinted that she would gain weight as she grew older. An expensive bracelet and a richly embroidered gown of heavy taffeta silk indicate her love of luxury, and her enormous ruff and high-crowned hat were so stylish she might be considered slightly ahead of her time. There was no primness in her face, but her serious expression and the firm set of her thin lips may have shown more than her husband intended to reveal. She took a solemn, no-nonsense approach to life that was typical of the Flemish middle class; her home and her family were her primary interests, and she devoted herself exclusively to them. Politics meant nothing to her, although she may have appreciated her husband's success as a diplomat. Her opinion of him as a painter is difficult to determine, but she was always fully clad when she posed for his portraits, even though Rubens' nudes became renowned throughout the civilized world.

There can be little doubt that the dashing, ambitious artist and his young wife were deeply in love, their mutual feeling symbolized in Rubens' first joint portrait by the way her hand covered his. Most of his colleagues were philanderers, and society granted them the privilege of living beyond the boundaries of the mores of the age, but no hint of scandal was ever attached to Rubens' name during the years of his marriage to Isabella Brandt. Whether he truly shared her sense of morality cannot be ascertained, but he loved her enough to accept her standards and to live accordingly.

The businessman-artist was as sedate as any Antwerp banker or merchant prince, and his wife made their home a luxuriously comfortable haven, a place where he could relax, and at the same time entertain in style when the occasion demanded. Philip Rubens the younger is the authority for the information that his Aunt Isabella set a table that became famous in a city known for its love of good food served in large quantities. When the artist and his wife dined alone, their nephew wrote, they ate meals of four or five courses; when guests were present, the menu was expanded, and nine or ten courses were customary. It is small wonder that both Peter Paul and Isabella became plump.

The couple had three children. The eldest was Clara Serena, who was baptized on March 21, 1611, and who died twelve years later, a victim of the plague that continued to sweep Europe at intervals. Her father adored her and was so crushed by her death that no one else ever took her place in his affections. The elder of his sons was Albert, diplomatically named after the regent, who was baptized on June 5, 1614, and lived to the age of forty-three. He showed no talent as a painter but did inherit his father's flair for politics, and was so able that he succeeded Peter Paul Rubens as Secretary to the Privy Council, a position of great honor that was not lacking in influence. The third child of the marriage was Nicolas, baptized on March 23, 1618, about whom the least is known and who died at the age of thirty-seven. He became a banker and lived quietly, achieving no particular prominence in business or social circles.

As was customary during the period, Isabella was primarily responsible for rearing the children, but her husband paid far more attention to his children than did most fathers of the time. Peter Paul Rubens had been exceptionally close to his own disgraced father during the decade prior to Jan Rubens' untimely death, and the painter not only set aside an hour each day to play with his children, read to them, and deliver lectures based on the Ten Commandments, but he closely supervised their education. It is noteworthy that none inherited his genius or became artists, although the sons of many Flemish painters almost automatically followed in the footsteps of their fathers. Perhaps Rubens' talent and renown were so overwhelming that his children were intimidated and knew that anything they might accomplish in his realm would be inferior.

It is significant that Rubens' domestic life adhered so closely to the middle-class norms of his era. His own childhood having been blighted by his father's scandalous behavior, he made certain that his own conduct was impeccable at all times, and he saved his emotional outbursts for expression on his canvases. His self-control would not have permitted him to do otherwise.

XI

The "Adoration of the Magi," the first painting by Peter Paul Rubens to be commissioned for permanent exhibition in Antwerp, did not remain in the city for more than a short time. It was unveiled in the Town Hall late in April, 1610, and only two years later was so admired by the Count of Oliva, the Spanish ambassador, that the city fathers deemed it wise to present it to him as a gift. The better part of a decade later the count conspired against the Spanish crown, his earthly goods were confiscated, and the painting came into the possession of King Philip IV. Then, when Rubens visited Madrid in 1628, he himself enlarged the work, adding a number of angels above the central figures, along with a procession of Magi, amusing himself by including his own portrait.

A number of authorities believe that the addition spoiled the unity of the work and unfavorably compare the enlarged version, now on exhibition in the Prado, Madrid, with the artist's careful sketch, which belongs to the Gemeente Museum of Groningen. The theme of the "Adoration" became one of Rubens' favorites, and he returned to it many times throughout his career. The finest of them, now the property of the Antwerp Museum, was done in 1624 for the Abbey of St. Michael; others include a large work, painted in 1620, that belongs to the Royal Museum in Brussels, one that was executed around 1619 for St.-Jean-de-Malines, and one painted in 1634 for a chapel in Louvain that found its permanent home at King's College, Cambridge.

As Rubens settled into the life of a painter in Flanders, his eloquent expressionism solidified in the style that now became his own. The overly elaborate influences of the Romans disappeared, and although he would remain indebted to Michelangelo, Titian, and Caravaggio for the rest of his life, his work was so dynamic, so filled with life, so overwhelming in scale yet so realistic in concept that it became uniquely his own. His genius was so all-encompassing that he established his own school and was copied by countless imitators, none of whom could match his ability to blend so many closely observed figures into a single, harmonious whole. The scope of his major work was so vast that other, lesser men lacked the imagination, much less the talent to match it. His dazzling combination of realism, romanticism, and expressionism set him apart.

The "Adoration" that was placed on exhibition in the Antwerp Town Hall, coming on the heels of Rubens' appointment as the court painter of the regents, won him first place in the eyes of his peers, and the public was not far behind in recognizing him as the greatest of living artists in the Low Countries. He was inundated with more orders than even a man who was forced to hire a large company of assistants and apprentices could handle, and his lifelong financial security was assured.

Rubens' style of living expanded accordingly. About two years after his marriage he bought a substantial stone dwelling, making a number of alterations, and through the years he added new wings until it became the Maison de Rubens that so many tourists have visited over the centuries. In his own day it was a large middle-class dwelling and was not considered ostentatious, but posterity has chosen to regard it as a small palace.

In all, it contained about forty rooms, including several salons, a huge dining hall and two large kitchens, a handsomely appointed library and more than a score of bedchambers. Since as many as six or eight apprentices lived with the family at any one time, it is unlikely that Rubens and Isabella thought they had many rooms to spare.

The artist's studio, which was located on the top floor, was the largest single room in the house and had a huge glass skylight that was made to his own specifications. Succeeding generations are in the debt of Van Dyck, who served as one of Rubens' assistants before striking out on his own: he painted the studio as he saw it on a typical day, and it was a barren place, devoid of draperies or wall decorations that might distract the master and his helpers. The only furniture consisted of a few plain tables and ordinary, straight-backed chairs, all of them unpadded. What dominated the chamber were several easels, all of them in use simultaneously.

When visitors came to the studio—and it was customary for men of prominence to drop in for a chat, even when they were not ordering portraits—they sat on the hard chairs or a bench placed near a long wall. No refreshments were offered in the studio, and someone in search of a glass of wine, a bit of cheese, or even dried herring was obliged to go elsewhere. Rubens was willing to adhere to the customs of the time and keep his doors open when he was at work, but he refused to encourage loiterers. His studio was a place where men worked for long hours without respite, and no one—including distinguished members of the nobility—was permitted to upset the disciplined routines.

In the many living rooms and corridors of the house Rubens was free to find expression for his great love of antiquity, and he collected so many busts, statues, and ornaments made by the Greeks and Romans that the house resembled a museum. He was influenced, to be sure, by the princes and prelates whose palaces he had visited in Italy, but his own taste was so unerring that, long before his death, his treasures far outstripped in both financial value and artistic worth the collections of many of the mighty.

Rubens' own favorite portion of the house was the inner courtyard, which had no roof. Here Isabella planted her gardens of flowers, herbs, and vegetables, and here her husband's admiration for the ancients knew no bounds. Moretus, in attempting to describe the courtyard in summer, found it impossible to restrain his own lyricism. There were Corinthian and Doric columns imported from Greece, marble busts on pedestals, and small statues of alabaster or marble everywhere. Flowers of every hue grew in disciplined profusion, and the air was heavy with their scent. Green vines grew up the columns, groupings of plants and statues set off small fountains, and the few visitors who were permitted to sample the delights of the courtyard were invited to help themselves to any fruits or flowers that struck their fancy.

Rubens and Isabella spent at least an hour or two in the garden each day, sitting on stone benches the artist designed himself, and favored guests shared their pleasure. Small children were excluded from the courtyard, however, and were not permitted to set foot in it until they were old enough not to trample the flowers or knock busts from their pedestals.

The artist's increasing wealth enabled him to live in a manner cultivated by great nobles, but his own standards remained unchanged. Granted that his clothes were fashioned of the finest cloth, but he never took time to visit a tailor, and Isabella probably saw to it that the artisan who came to the Rubens' house to measure the master for new breeches, doublet, or shoes did not interfere with the master's work schedule.

Rubens ate what was regarded as a small breakfast, usually a grilled fish, cheese, and fruit. He took his noon meal in his studio, and his assistants sometimes complained that they, too, were forced to subsist on bread, cheese, and watered wine eaten while they continued to work. Although daylight was a precious commodity that Rubens could not allow himself to squander, he was so in love with Isabella that, weather permitting, he made the time to join her in the garden each day for a quiet chat. What they discussed is not known and has been the subject of endless speculation.

At sundown the day's work in the studio ended, but Rubens retired to a small, bare chamber located near the bedroom he shared with his wife and continued to labor by candlelight, which was sufficiently strong for him to make the carefully executed sketches that he always drew prior to beginning a major painting. How long he closeted himself in seclusion depended upon the sense of pressure he felt, but he rarely stopped work for the day until he spent two or three hours there.

Dinner was a time for relaxation. Isabella and Peter Paul, when dining alone, consumed a thick soup, followed by fish, fowl, and meat, usually in that order and, more often than not, ended their meal with a honey-sweetened dessert, sometimes fruit that had been cooked in wine and honey. Husband and wife both drank sparingly, although their wine cellar was renowned as one of the best in Antwerp and a visitor who hoped to persuade the master to paint his portrait was advised to bring him a gift of a foreign wine.

Moretus, who dined at the Rubens' home more often than anyone except Peter Paul's brothers and their families, wrote that the artist rarely seemed to note what he was consuming. He was a compulsive talker who was interested in the whole world of his era, and when a visitor could contribute to his knowledge he bombarded the man with questions throughout the meal. He was quick to become aware of any dish that was not prepared to his liking, however, and when he took only a token bite or two, Isabella had the offending dish removed and another substituted for it. Moretus also wrote that when Rubens was at work on a major painting his appetite suffered, and rather than eat rich dishes that might upset his digestion he consumed only bread, cheese, and dried fish, drinking small quantities of watered wine with his meal. But he insisted that everyone else eat the delicacies that had been prepared under Isabella's strict supervision by the family's cooks, and he was hurt if guests did not enjoy the fare. It did not bother him, however, to subsist on a Spartan diet, even when others were eating dishes that he regarded as his favorites when free from pressure.

The *Vita Rubenii* reveals that Rubens required less rest than most men, which may explain, to some extent, why he was able to produce such an enormous body of work. No matter how he might occupy himself during the evening, he rarely retired before midnight, and then spent an hour or two reading before he dropped off to sleep. He was always awake shortly before dawn, and when the sun came up, he was already in his studio, impatiently waiting to begin his day's work as soon as he could see what he was doing.

In the nineteenth century it became fashionable for the detractors of Eugène Delacroix to denigrate him by attacking Rubens as a man who put on airs and tried to live above his station. Delacroix, one of the great artists of his own age, was inclined to identify with Rubens, in part because of his own clouded paternity; it was rumored that he was the illegitimate son of Talleyrand, the great Austrian diplomat.

The problems faced by Delacroix have no place here, but the assaults on Rubens are not substantiated by known facts.

Only in one respect are the claims valid. It was the custom in Flanders, as it was elsewhere in Europe, for no one but members of the nobility to carry swords. By no stretch of even Rubens' own elastic imagination had he been born into the nobility, and many years would pass before two monarchs gave him places in their respective peerages. All the same, he had carried a sword since his years in Italy, and the hilt of a full-length dress sword is prominently displayed in his portrait of himself and Isabella Brandt.

So there can be no question that he was assuming a prerogative to which he was not entitled. His airs were harmless, however, and were overlooked by everyone who knew him. If he was something of an eccentric and wanted to pretend he was a diplomat and a nobleman, his friends were probably amused, and the constabulary had no intention of arresting a man who enjoyed the favor of the Archduke Albert and of the Flemish bishops. Ultimately Rubens enjoyed the last laugh at the expense of critics who would follow him into the world by three hundred years.

No matter how handsome his home or how expensive the fabrics from which his clothes were cut, his business sense never deserted him. Nowhere is this better illustrated than in the attitude he displayed when he gained overnight popularity and was flooded with more offers of commissions than he could accept. He could charge private clients high fees only in proportion to his increasing reputation, and the best way to accomplish that goal could be found through the Church, the single most important art patron of the age. So, except for his flattering, somewhat idealized portrait of the Archduke Albert and the Archduchess Isabella, Rubens built his name by regretfully postponing private offers and concentrating on religious paintings ordered for church ornamentation by wealthy bishops, priests, and abbots. It has been estimated that more than seventy-five percent of his work over a five-year period after he established himself in Antwerp was in the form of Church commissions.

His many paintings of Albert, Isabella, and various high-ranking members of their court, which can be found in a number of European galleries, can be classified as technical masterpieces, painted without feeling. Here was Rubens at his efficient best, doing what he deemed necessary, but he did no more than fulfill his obligation to his sponsors. His heart lay elsewhere.

Not even the assistants who worked with him could relieve the pressures, so great were the demands for his services. In May, 1611, he sent a letter to Jacques de Brie, a Brussels engraver who had recommended a talented young assistant to him, and his candor offers the best explanation of his situation:

> I am so besieged that there are apprentices who have been waiting for years, under other masters, for me to be able to accept them. Truly, and without exaggeration, I have found it necessary to turn away more than one hundred aspirants, among them blood relatives and the sons of lifelong friends. Could your young candidate serve his apprenticeship elsewhere, I might better be able to find a place in my studio for him as a journeyman, it being somewhat more difficult to persuade graduate painters to remain in my service.

Gradually, as Rubens' ever-expanding practice made it unnecessary for him to devote as much of his time to the Church and the regents, Rubens accepted an order from any client who could pay his exceptionally high prices. He became known as a man who would reject no substantial offer, and he turned out portraits and paintings on religious and mythical themes in huge quantities. The scope of his work is astonishing. In the Louvre hangs the model for an even larger painting in the Prado, "Philopeomen, General of the Acheans, Recognized by an Old Woman," and nowhere is his superb Baroque style more evident. At the same time he did the "Annunciation," now the property of the Kunsthistoriches Museum, and a "Samson and Delilah" sketch, now hanging in Chicago's Art Institute. He also did a "Brazen Serpent," which is in a private English collection, and two major works for the Church of St. Paul in Antwerp, an "Adoration of the Shepherds" and an even more impressive masterpiece, the "Glorification of the Holy Sacrament by the Church Fathers." This great work was inspired by Raphael's *Disputà*, which Rubens had seen in the Vatican, and he freely acknowledged his debt to the earlier master.

These efforts alone were of such great variety that it is difficult to believe they were the accomplishments of one man, but that is only the beginning of the story of Rubens' industry. In June, 1610, the Antwerp Church Council, supported by a prominent art patron, Cornelius van der Geest, ordered a triptych from Rubens for the high altar of the Church of St. Walburge. It was to be called the "Raising of the Cross," and the finished work would be hailed as one of the most magnificent ever painted by any artist.

Rubens was so anxious to start work on this commission that he began it during a brief period, after moving out of his old house and taking up residence in the new, when he and Isabella stayed with his father-in-law. He transferred his canvas to his new home, then finished the painting in the church itself, so it would fit precisely into its surroundings. Never again would he knowingly commit the error that had caused him such problems in Rome.

Apparently all Antwerp knew he was working on an immortal masterpiece. Friends and strangers came to his studio in such vast numbers to watch him as he worked that he was forced to assign one of his apprentices the duties of doorkeeper, and only those coming to see him on legitimate business were admitted. When art lovers still found excuses to sneak in, Isabella Brandt intervened, and her threat to close the doors of the new house to everyone finally won her husband some measure of the privacy he required. During the final stages of composition the church was filled with great crowds, so the dock workers of Antwerp voluntarily constructed a huge screen of canvas that shielded the painter and his work from his admirers.

It is no exaggeration that the difficulties encountered by Rubens in painting the "Raising of the Cross" were responsible for the creation of his new studio, which was forty feet long and thirty feet wide. Never again, if he could help it, would he be forced to suffer inconvenience when at work on a large project.

Little by little, as the artist's fame increased, he was compelled to change his work habits. He installed a reception room on the far side of the arched entrance to his studio, and his visitors were asked to wait for him there. By the time he reached middle age his house was filled with so many valuable statues and paintings that he had no room for them anywhere but in the studio itself, and two walls were filled with them.

Other austerities also disappeared. A rich cloth covered the main table in the studio, padded chairs replaced more Spartan furniture, and several carved, inlaid cabinets designed by the master housed completed canvases.

In spite of Rubens' frugal meals he continued to gain weight, and several years before Isabella Brandt's untimely death she was successful in persuading her husband to become more active physically. Thereafter he stopped work at sundown and went out for a canter beyond the city walls on one of the blooded Spanish horses he kept in his stable. For the rest of his life he rode daily, regardless of whether he was in Antwerp or making a visit to a foreign land.

He also gave up his practice of making sketches after

dark, and the eyestrain caused by his profession was so severe that he hired a young student to read to him from the classics while he worked. He took up the hobby of collecting coins, medals, and marble samples, and was as compulsively energetic in the pursuit of his avocation as he was zealous in his ambition to become the greatest painter of his age. His collection of coins, medals, and marbles became the largest in Europe, and he spent hours every evening rearranging them and classifying new additions.

He gave Isabella Brandt full credit for this relaxation from his labors. His nephew, writing in the *Vita Rubenii*, writes that Rubens frequently remarked that a man deserved a little time for simple pleasures at the end of a fourteen-hour day. Only Peter Paul Rubens would rise at four o'clock in the morning, attend mass, and be ready to start work at five. But, he contended, it was necessary for him to compensate in some way for the "frivolous" pleasures, as he called them in a letter to Moretus, that occupied him after he completed a day of work.

His industry was a never-ending source of astonishment to everyone who knew him, and not even the wife he loved could persuade him to rest. Only on Sundays did he consent to follow a slightly more relaxed schedule, stopping work in midafternoon to take his place at the head of a dinner table crowded with relatives and friends.

As Rubens grew older, his interests became more far-ranging. He was fascinated by physics and set up a small laboratory in his home so he could conduct experiments. His lifelong interest in mythology led to his absorption in astronomy, and he mounted a powerful glass made for him at the university of Louvain so he could study the stars. He also became interested in the microscope, invented in his own day in the Low Countries by Anton van Leeuwenhoek.

In 1611 Johannes Kepler published the basic principles of the compound microscope named after him, and this instrument, which was built in 1628 by Christoph Scheiner, startled the scientists of Europe. Rubens shared in the excitement, and in 1630 he acquired a microscope of his own, constructed for him at Louvain at great expense. A typical Renaissance man, the artist who became the symbol of all that was good in the Counter-Reformation had a thirst for knowledge in every realm. His interests were so broad that the real miracle of Peter Paul Rubens is that he found time for his painting.

XII

In the "Raising of the Cross" Rubens provided a definitive answer to a question that was perplexing some of the most learned theologians of his day. Was Christ nailed to a cross lying on the ground, or was the cross already erect when He was nailed to it? His decision was based on artistic rather than theological grounds, and his great painting, in which suffering and fury, horror and pain and passion were expressed with such dynamic force and lyricism, settled the controversy.

Aware of the delicacy of the ground on which he was treading, Rubens submitted his preliminary sketch to the bishops and lesser members of the clergy, to the Archduke Albert's deputy for Antwerp, to the members of the local aristocracy, and finally, wanting an expression of opinion from the people who would see his work, to any citizen of Antwerp who felt inclined to offer a comment.

There were some, clergy and laymen alike, who were repelled by the brutality and violence of Rubens' interpretation, but the majority were moved by the tenderness and agony of the central figures, and agreed with Rubens. The vigor of his execution matched the power of his theme, and his daring in discarding the moderation that had always been characteristic of religious themes was equalled by his daring in execution. He presented an off-balance composition in his center panel, and his use of the diagonal was little less than extraordinary.

He made many sketches before he attacked the painting itself, and although some of these works have been lost, others may be found in collections in Vienna, Berlin, Oxford, and New York. Rubens undoubtedly realized he was attempting something very new and different, and he worked with a care equal to his zeal.

His finished work, which marked his almost complete break with the Roman school, created a sensation. It was too strong for the moderate Flemings, and even those prominent clergymen and nobles who had applauded his original sketch now drew back from it. No one could decry the power and fury of his work, but his daring left the contemporary viewer dazed, and while the "Raising of the Cross" elevated Rubens to a stature far above that of any other artist of his time, he was criticized for having gone too far.

The great painting, it might be noted, remained in the church for which it had been painted until 1794, when it was taken to Paris. Returned to Antwerp in 1815, after the fall of Napoleon I, it now may be seen in the Antwerp Cathedral.

In 1611, soon after Rubens completed the "Raising of the Cross," he received a new commission for a matching work from the gunsmiths of Antwerp for their chapel in the Antwerp Cathedral. The "Descent from the Cross" took far longer to execute: The center panel was delivered late in 1612, more than a year after the painter began the enterprise, and the side panels were not completed until the winter of 1614. He was busy on a variety of other enterprises during this time.

Elegant and powerful in its own right, the "Descent" deserves to be called a masterpiece, too, but it is far narrower in its ideas and execution, conforming far more closely to the more conservative demands of the Counter-Reformation. It has been said that Rubens demonstrated an uneven quality in the development of his own style, and the "Descent," in which he returns to the Italian approach he had abandoned in the "Raising," is used as irrefutable evidence of this contention.

It is impossible for the claim to be denied. At the same time, however, Rubens was totally dependent upon the clergy and the nobility for his livelihood. No one knew better than he how fragile a man's reputation could be. No man better understood that he would be ruined if he underestimated the ultimate power of the bishops and the high-ranking nobles.

Regardless of the stature he had already attained, the reputation that was bringing him offers from every part of Europe, he would be destroyed if he ignored the criticism of the wealthy who held the real reins of power in their manicured hands.

No work of art was the exclusive product of the artist. A wealthy patron usually indicated in some detail what he wanted included and omitted from his portrait. And a major work of art was subject to many influences. Nicholas Rockox played an important role in obtaining Rubens' commission for the "Descent," and the powerful Rockox, who had his own ideas about art, was conservative in his taste and judgments. Certainly he would not have been a man to offend with impunity.

The gunsmiths held a guild meeting and voted unanimously in favor of the inclusion of their patron, St. Christopher, in the center panel of the triptych. But this decision did not rest lightly with the Flemish bishops, who called a synod in the late autumn of 1611 for the purpose of weighing the question.

After due deliberation behind closed doors, they countermanded the order of the gunsmiths. Only Christ, they ruled, could occupy the center of altar paintings. So St. Christopher was banished to the exterior of one of the wings. This decision, which was made in secret—no word on the proceedings has ever been made public, down to the present day—was final, and there was no appeal.

Rubens had favored the idea presented to him by the gunsmiths, but he was compelled to accept the bishops' ruling. The great cathedral was a part of their domain, and he knew they would not accept the painting or authorize payment by the gunsmiths if he chose to defy them. Rubens was wise enough to take the hint and retreated toward the conservatism that had marked religious paintings for so long a time.

The "Descent from the Cross" had been portrayed by countless artists, all of whom had observed a number of unwritten rules. For more than two hundred years these conventions had been rigid, but in 1541 a painting done in Rome by Daniele de Volterra had set new precedents. Volterra's work was still regarded as too spectacular by some of the more reactionary elements of the Counter-Reformation, but he was almost universally regarded as respectable. Rubens, in electing to follow the lead of Volterra, showed that he was willing to abide by the rules, while at the same time demonstrating some measure of the independence of spirit that distinguished the true artist from the hack.

His Virgin Mary was his one unique contribution, serving notice that his willingness to compromise was limited. Neither Volterra nor any other painter had dared to defy the tradition, imposed by conservative bishops who had enjoyed the full support of the Papacy for more than a century, that Mary should always be portrayed as a woman endowed with strengths greater than those of mere humans. The Mary who was depicted by Rubens in the "Descent" was a figure of great dignity and tenderness—but was completely human. He showed her as a weeping, tragic figure, obviously suffering, as she stretched out a hand in the direction of the limp body of her son.

Rubens' mastery of his medium made it impossible for even the most conservative of contemporary theologians to take offense, however, and his portrayal was not criticized. It was impossible to deny his own religious devotion, and the spiritual quality of the "Descent" was so intense that the great painting won him still more recognition as a genius.

One of the most striking figures in the "Descent" is Mary Magdalene, seen in profile, and her face has a haunting, ethereal beauty that is extraordinary, making her one of the most memorable women Rubens ever painted.

The success of the "Descent" was immediate, and Rubens received more requests for other works on the same theme than he was physically capable of handling. Over the years he supervised the painting of several more versions of the "Descent," and no two were identical. In these labors he received the assistance of the skilled painters who worked with him, but it is not true that his helpers did all of the work and that he merely signed various paintings. Any completed canvas that emerged from the studio of Peter Paul Rubens usually was his own; others might handle backgrounds and various details of composition, but the major figures often were his alone.

The men who worked with Rubens in his studio were no mere apprentices, and a number of them were recognized as masters in their own right. Perhaps his most remarkable association was that which he enjoyed with Jan Bruegel, the second son of Pieter Bruegel the Elder. Nine years older than Rubens and already an artist of established reputation when Rubens returned to Antwerp from Italy, Jan Bruegel soon merged his own talents with those of the man whose extraordinary genius he was quick to recognize. Known to his contemporaries as "Velvet" Bruegel because of his fondness for painting shimmering, luxurious folds of rich cloth, the older man had followed in the footsteps of his father and brother, but his own success had been limited because of his fondness for landscapes and religious scenes. He had painted few portraits and, as a consequence, had never enjoyed much popularity. But he found his niche in the Rubens studio and remained with Rubens until his death in 1625.

Frans Snyders was another who seemed to fit perfectly into Rubens' studio. A man whose work habits were similar to those of his good friend and master, Snyders' one great flaw was a lack of imagination. But no detail was too small to escape his loving attention, and his style was so similar to that of Rubens that his contributions blended into the whole harmoniously. Snyders, an expert in the painting of animals, spent the better part of his long career working as one of Rubens' principal assistants, although—like a number of others—he also did independent work under his own name.

The most important of Rubens' associations was one that lasted only a few years before the young man went out on his own initiative to become a great painter. Anthony Van Dyck, the son of a wealthy silk merchant, was twenty-two years younger than Rubens and was a child of nine when Rubens returned to Antwerp from Italy. The following year the little boy, who was destined to become the second most prominent Flemish painter of the seventeenth century, began his apprenticeship with another painter.

The precise date of his entry into the Rubens' household is unknown, but most authorities agree that he may have become one of Rubens' apprentices as early as 1613, when he was only fourteen years of age. It has been established that he remained with Rubens until late in 1620, almost three years after he attained his own standing as a master in the Antwerp guild.

Rubens was the first to recognize and encourage Van Dyck's genius, and in 1618 he offered a painting by his disciple to the British ambassador in the Netherlands, calling Van Dyck "my best pupil." By 1620 Van Dyck's reputation was becoming widespread, and according to one prominent correspondent of the period, his work "is appreciated in Antwerp as much as is that of Rubens himself."

This claim was something of an exaggeration, to be sure, but Rubens showed no jealousy of his assistant's growing stature. On the contrary, he was instrumental in obtaining a number of independent commissions for his former apprentice, thereby enabling Van Dyck to establish his own studio. Late in 1620, when the two men parted company, Rubens gave Van Dyck glowing letters of introduction to a number of wealthy art patrons in England, and thanks to his help, the younger painter's path was smoothed.

By 1618, perhaps as early as the preceding year, Van Dyck's rapidly developing style became distinctly his own. So it may be unfair to call him Rubens' assistant during their final years together. It might be more accurate to refer to their association as a collaboration.

The fact that these two geniuses worked together for a number of years has fascinated posterity, and a number of legends have come into being regarding their relationship, most of them false. It has been said for three hundred and fifty years that Rubens was jealous of the independent success achieved by Van Dyck, but there is no basis in fact for this assertion, even though Van Dyck painted the portraits of many people who might have gone to Rubens had they not offered commissions to his former disciple.

The pair remained close at least until 1630, and after that

time they drifted apart, although their personal relations remained cordial. Rubens could not have been jealous of Van Dyck, nor had he any reason to place obstacles in the younger man's path. The truth of the matter is that Peter Paul Rubens, from the time of his first major successes in Antwerp—in 1609 and 1610, when Van Dyck was still a child—had more offers of work than it was physically possible for him to accept. His frantically busy career, both as a painter and as a diplomat, made it necessary for him to reject offers that other, lesser men craved. So he probably accepted the success of Van Dyck with relief and pleasure.

The reputation of Peter Paul Rubens was so great and so widespread by the time Anthony Van Dyck emerged as an independent painter in his own right that there was no reason for the older man to feel jealous of his former apprentice. It must be remembered, too, that Rubens' fame was based on his achievements in virtually every field of painting, while Van Dyck's growing standing rested almost exclusively on his skill as painter of portraits and religious subjects. Only in this realm did they "compete," but there was more than enough room in Europe for both men to function.

On the personal side, unfounded rumors about the supposed licentiousness of the exceptionally handsome though short Van Dyck have abounded for centuries. These have been based, in part, on the fact that in 1620, shortly before he parted company with Rubens, Van Dyck sired an illegitimate child. He not only acknowledged his paternity, but when the mother proved incompetent, he took custody of the infant—a girl whom he named Maria Theresa. She was reared by his sister, a pious woman who spent many years in a convent, although she never took final vows. Van Dyck saw his daughter frequently, keeping up the relationship after his marriage only two years prior to his death. He left a substantial estate to his sister for the benefit of Maria

Theresa, and a number of letters he wrote to the girl over the years are still extant, amply demonstrating his devotion to her.

How Rubens reacted when he learned that Van Dyck had sired an illegitimate daughter is unknown, but the news in no way harmed his affection for the younger man. Inasmuch as many painters led freer lives than did most of their contemporaries, it is unlikely that the Rubens was surprised.

One of the more persistent legends about the two painters portrays them as homosexual lovers, perhaps because of their closeness despite the difference in their ages. This charge must be regarded as absurd. If Van Dyck indulged in homosexual relationships at any time in his life that fact has never been proved, and it is highly unlikely that Rubens, who loved women so ardently and may have done more than any other artist in history to glorify the feminine figure, engaged in an active homosexual life. His enemies would have been delighted to pounce on any evidence that would have tarnished his name, and in a community as small as Antwerp it would have been difficult—if not impossible—to keep such an affair secret.

Both master and apprentice were living under the same roof, to be sure, but it must not be forgotten that the very moral Isabella Brandt Rubens, who was devoted to her husband and was deeply loved in return, also lived there. Therefore, these rumors, which are totally lacking in any demonstrable foundation, must be dismissed as nonsense.

What is far more important is that Van Dyck's skills as an artist were developed under the tutelage of Rubens, as were those of many others. At no time during Rubens' career as a mature artist did he employ fewer than three or four apprentices and perhaps an equal number of senior assistants who themselves held qualifications as masters.

The operation was unique in its own day, and lesser

artists, envying the success of the man whose brilliance relegated them to the shadows, loved to refer to the Rubens studio as "an art factory" where third-rate painters mechanically pieced together their joint efforts. These assaults were meaningless, however, as was recognized in Rubens' own day. His touch was unmistakable and could be seen on every canvas that left his studio under his name.

He made all of the original sketches, then blocked out the painting itself. At that point his assistants took over, filling in backgrounds and details under the ever-watchful eye of the master, who reserved the more important portions of the painting for himself.

One of the more remarkable aspects of the Rubens operation was its harmony. Creative artists are supposedly men of erratic temperament and unpredictable moods, but the disciplined Rubens rarely allowed himself the indulgence of his own feelings, and those who worked with him followed his example. No member of the entourage lost sight of the fact that he was a well-paid member of a highly successful business enterprise, and everyone acted accordingly. There can be little doubt that Rubens was an able, conscientious executive who would have been a success in any field he had chosen to enter.

XIII

One day in the early autumn of 1612 Philip Rubens was acting as chairman of a meeting in the council room of the Antwerp Town Hall. In the midst of a lively debate on a matter of some municipal consequence he arose and began to make an attempt to reconcile the positions of the two opposing factions. Suddenly he paused, a surprised expression crossing his face, and then he slumped to the floor, dead of a heart attack at the age of thirty-eight. The shock of his passing was so great that his widow lost her sanity, and a short time later she also died.

Peter Paul Rubens grieved for the brother he had loved, and before the end of the year he formally adopted his brother's two small children, Philip and Clara. They moved into the mansion that was always large enough to accommodate more people, and thereafter Rubens and Isabella treated the children as their own. Clara grew up to marry a minor member of the nobility who would make a distinguished career for himself as a general, and Philip the younger, the most ambitious of his contemporaries, studied for the law, eventually became a municipal administrator, following in the footsteps of his father and grandfather, and then developed literary ambitions as well. His *Vita Rubenii* was only one of a number of books he wrote; the most popular was an inaccurate but colorful history of Flanders, and another was a history of the Netherlands' House of Orange, which was subsidized by Prince John William of that family.

Peter Paul Rubens assumed financial responsibility for the children of his sister, Blandine, too, when the death of their father, Du Parcq, left them penniless in 1615 or 1616. As far as is known, however, these youngsters, now adolescents, did not move in with him and Isabella. Rubens' only surviving brother was the eldest, Jan-Baptiste, who was self-sufficient and needed no financial assistance from the successful artist. Little is known of their relationship; they had never been particularly close, and since they moved in different spheres, it has been assumed that they saw relatively little of each other. Occasionally Peter Paul referred casually in his correspondence to the presence under his roof of Jan-Baptiste and his family on a holiday or feast day, when it appears the brothers maintained some sort of token relationship. No information is available on the year of Jan-Baptiste's death, and nothing is known about the lives and careers of his children. If their renowned uncle played an active role in their lives, the facts have been concealed from posterity.

Some facts regarding Rubens' own life demonstrate the steadfastness of his loyalty to old friends. No matter how great his fame, he always made the time to draw elaborate pencil sketches for the title pages of books published by Moretus, and a mutual friend, Theodore Galle, made the engravings. Rubens drew scores of such sketches through the years, and although other publishers gladly would have paid him a small fortune for similar work, he refused to accept more than token sums from Moretus. By far the most prominent member of the Guild of St. Luke, Rubens also was influential in persuading various colleagues to send their engraving work to Galle.

As a gesture to various friends, the artist also designed chandeliers, chests of drawers, and other furniture; and the superb craftsmen of Antwerp carefully followed his specifications. There was such a great demand for one crystal chandelier in particular that Rubens established a profitable side venture in 1620 or thereabouts. He and two merchants went into business together, the latter supplying the capital and Rubens providing the designs for various items of furniture. Patents and copyrights were virtually unknown, however, and Rubens' designs were copied so widely in so many countries that the company was disbanded after a few years. All the same, Rubens and his partners earned a handsome profit from the enterprise, and the bankers of Antwerp gravely approved of the artist who had a Midas touch.

It was during the early part of the second decade of the seventeenth century that Rubens formed his long association with Sir Dudley Carleton, the British ambassador at The Hague, who was a close friend and protégé of the powerful Duke of Buckingham. An art patron of note, Carleton long had collected ancient Greek and Roman statuary and, having developed an appetite for Flemish paintings and tapestries, got in touch with Rubens.

There was nothing the painter wanted more than fine marbles for his home, and the two men conducted negotiations that lasted for months. Eventually they reached an agreement, and Rubens, who purchased the tapestries from a friend for two thousand gold florins, was convinced that he was the better bargainer because he received one of Europe's finest collections of marbles. But it was Sir Dudley who really won: Rubens included some of his own paintings, several of which he painted expressly for the purpose of inclusion in the deal, and within a few generations they were beyond price.

Meanwhile Rubens' studio continued to grow. He was joined by Deodate del Monte, his old friend from his Italian days, and by two accomplished landscape painters, Jan Wildens and Lucas van Uden, who worked under the direction of Bruegel. The "factory" was operating at capacity.

With the "Descent from the Cross" behind him and his respectability in theological circles reestablished, Rubens felt free to paint as he wished. He did a small altarpiece, "The Resurrection," which was placed in the cathedral above the tomb of Moretus' uncle, and then, in a flurry of activity, he went on to a number of nonreligious works. These included a "Jupiter and Callisto," now in the Cassel Museum, and a related painting, "Venus, Bacchus and Ceres," now in the collection of the same museum. Both of these works were dated 1613 and were signed. His amusing "Victory over Drunkenness and Lust" was done at approximately the same time, and is now in the Kunsthistorisches Museum. Soon thereafter he painted "Cupid Making His Arrow," perhaps a copy or an adaptation of an Italian painting, now the property of the Schleissheim Museum.

It is significant that, although these works are done in Rubens' own Baroque style, the Italian approach again having been rejected, his themes were solidly conservative and reflected the middle-class views of respectable Antwerp. Rubens, the moralist, decried everything that was frivolous in human nature.

Two prominent religious paintings were done by Rubens in 1613: "The Holy Family" and "The Virgin with Parrot." The former is now in the Pitti Palace and the latter in the Antwerp Museum. Rubens himself regarded both as distinctly "minor" works, and it may be that this was the reason he again used the free, bold approach that was his own version of the works of Caravaggio. His "Hero Crowned by Victory," now in the Cassel Museum, soon followed, and is significant because it includes the torso of a blonde woman, seen from the rear, that is regarded as Rubens' ideal female figure.

He painted so many masterpieces in 1614 that no enumeration of the major works can do them justice. There were:

The "Flight into Egypt," now at Cassel, one of a number he painted on this same theme. A lesser version, done on a wood panel, may be seen in Lisbon.

"Susanna and the Elders," now in the National Museum, Stockholm, that subsequently was recognized as one of his greatest works. It is one of many on the same Biblical theme and shows Susanna, who has been bathing her feet in a spring, hastily trying to cover her body with a sheet when she is surprised by the elders. This is one of the very few works that Rubens both signed and dated. In all, it is believed that Rubens painted six versions of "Susanna"; one is lost, and only the sketch for it is extant.

Venus Frigida, a charming work now in the Antwerp Museum, is another that glorifies his buxom, idealized feminine figure. It was rumored that the unknown model who posed for this work was Rubens' mistress, but there is no concrete evidence to substantiate the assertion.

A *Pietà,* one of several, now in the Kunsthistorisches Museum.

As Peter Paul Rubens approached his fortieth birthday, it became increasingly obvious that he was the master of every field into which he ventured. He estimated that he was forced to reject three portrait requests for each commission he accepted. His boldness, his ability to walk the thin borderline of convention, might make the Church apprehensive, but bishops and priests all over Europe were anxious to obtain one of his works, and the time was rapidly approaching when he would be in a position to make his own rules with impunity. Until then, he was flooded with many more offers of commissions from prelates than he could accept. His so-called mythological studies—in reality paintings of his own age which were loosely set on a mythological stage—were so popular that he refused to paint them on order and preferred to offer them to wealthy collectors and patrons only when he completed them.

Oddly, although 1615 was a busy year for Rubens, only one work done then bears his signature. It was a triptych, "Doubting Thomas," and Nicholas Rockox obtained the commission for Rubens from the Church of the Minorites in Antwerp. The side panels, which portray Rockox and his wife, Adrienne Perez, may have been added at a later date, and for a time were displayed above their tomb in the Church of the Minorites before the whole work was removed to the Antwerp Museum. Powerful in conception, this painting was nevertheless conventional, one of the last of the type that Rubens ever did.

Soon thereafter the artist launched permanently into the boldly Baroque style that had made the "Raising of the Cross" so spectacular. He was in frequent correspondence with Father Paolo da Cesana, the general of the Capuchins, who asked him to do "St. Francis Receiving the Stigmata." Some of the letters written by both men have been lost; this has created something of a mystery. Father da Cesana protested that Rubens' asking price of four hundred gold ducats was too high and claimed that the order could not afford to pay it. Rubens adopted a lofty tone that was, nevertheless, free of condescension. After hinting that he believed the Capuchins—reputedly one of the wealthiest orders in Europe—might find his price if they searched their treasury, he refused to lower his fee, saying that he charged branches of the Church far less than he charged private individuals, and that he expected to make only a small profit.

No one has ever learned, down to the present day, which of the principals finally gave in and accepted the price of the other. But that is only a sidelight. What is important is that Rubens did his "St. Francis," now included in a private collection in Belgium. In it and in his "Martyrdom of St. Ursula," which followed it and which is now in the Brussels Museum, he threw off the restraints of convention and proclaimed his own Baroque style for all time. From then until the end of his days his power and fury were spell-binding. His almost magical intensity enabled him to combine economy with hurricane force, and the results left the viewer speechless in admiration of his dazzling genius.

So the year 1616 may be the most important in his career; by now he had attained a stature that no cardinal or bishop could deny. The genius of Rubens was so universally recognized, as was his personal devotion to Christianity, that no churchman was willing to make a fool of himself by complaining about a Rubens painting, no matter what his own opinion of the work might be.

It was in 1616, too, that Balthasar Moretus commissioned the first of many superb paintings, commissions which extended over a period of more than five years. Among them were "Gaspar," "Melchior," and "Balthazar." Rubens' oldest and dearest friend wanted these works exhibited at his Plantin Press. A number of members of the Plantin and Moretus families were represented, along with a large gallery of the famous, selected jointly by Moretus and Rubens. These included such disparate persons as:

Plato
Seneca
Pope Leo X
Lorenzo de' Medici
King Alfonso of Aragon
King Mathias Corvinus of Hungary
Pico della Mirandola
Our Lady with the Infant Jesus
St. Gaspar

St. Melchior

St. Balthazar

In order to accomplish all that was required it became necessary for Rubens to expand the originally contemplated three paintings into five. He charged his old friend a below-cost price of thirty gold florins for each of the paintings, a total of one hundred and fifty florins for the entire task. Perhaps the price was so low because his students did much of the work. Nevertheless, anyone else would have been compelled to pay one hundred to one hundred and fifty florins for each painting.

This mammoth project represented a reversion to Rubens' "polite" style, which he found far easier for private clients to bear than the slashing attacks which marked his major works. The Moretus project is of special interest because it may have been the first in which Van Dyck had a hand. Even at this early stage of his career the younger painter was sufficiently individualistic to paint in his own way, and neither he nor Rubens, with all of their combined genius, could reconcile the two approaches. The result is somewhat uneven, but the Moretus Magi are priceless.

The confusion that was caused by the presence of Van Dyck in Rubens' studio still persists. For a long time a painting of the son of the Bey of Tunis, falsely called "Tammerlaine" since 1826, when it was exhibited in England, was long attributed to Van Dyck, but by the nineteenth century the authorities changed their minds and decided it had been painted by Rubens.

Even greater difficulty was encountered in determining the authorship of the study called "Four Negro Heads," a bold work that appears typical of the mature Rubens. The model for this work was a black sailor who visited Antwerp, possibly in 1618 or 1619, and the problem was caused by the fact that he also posed for Van Dyck and for Jordaens. "Four Negro Heads," which was in newspaper headlines throughout the world when it was stolen from the Brussels Museum in 1964, was believed, even then, to have been done by Van Dyck. Recovered intact within a few weeks, the painting thus called itself anew to the attention of various authorities, and it was as recently as 1965 that some of the world's leading art experts reversed previous judgments and declared that the painting had been done by Rubens.

The *"Christ à la Paille,"* which was commissioned by Nicolas Damant of the Council of Brabant for the Church of St. Gudule in Brussels was a powerful work which Rubens painted in 1616 or thereabouts and dedicated to Damant and his family. It is generally considered superior to "Christ Giving the Keys to St. Peter," which was done more or less simultaneously, and now hangs in the Wallace Collection in London. It has been impossible to determine the dates of a number of other important paintings done between 1614 and 1617. These include a "Virgin with the Sleeping Child," now in Munich, "Christ in the House of Simon," and another "Descent from the Cross."

Among the many Rubens paintings of the period done in the 1614–17 period the following are known:

"Adoration of the Magi," commissioned by the Capuchin Fathers of Tournai, now in the Brussels Museum.

"Christ and the Adulteress," also in the Brussels Museum.

"The Massacre of the Innocents," one of his more compellingly powerful works, which is yet another in the Brussels Museum.

"Virgin with a Basket," in Potsdam Schloss.

"The Child Jesus with St. John and Two Angels," now in the Kunsthistorisches Museum. This work was so popular in Rubens' own time that he himself made two splendid copies of it, receiving high fees for all three. The fact that the master himself made the copies, a most unusual procedure, was revealed by Philip the younger in the *Vita Rubenii,* and although he is sometimes inaccurate in relating details, there is no reason to doubt his word.

"The Flagellation," an exceptionally powerful work, which was commissioned by the Dominican Fathers for their Church of St. Paul in Antwerp, still hangs there today. The date, 1617, is inscribed on the side panels, but some authorities believe these figures were added some years later.

Three works were done in collaboration with Jan Bruegel: "Madonna and Child with a Garland," which now hangs in Munich; "The Madonna with a Garland," now in the Louvre; and "The Madonna with Forget-me-nots," now in Brussels. It is significant that Rubens tried hard to accommodate his style to that of the softer Bruegel, but these efforts were not completely successful. Bruegel himself recognized this, and in a letter to his old patron, Cardinal Borromeo, he remarked that it was impossible for his friend to conceal his strength when portraying the central figure of Mary.

The relationship of the two men was so close that it is worthy of further examination.

XIV

Peter Paul Rubens and Jan Bruegel were partners as well as friends, and their relationship, both professional and personal, well may be unique in the history of artists. In all probability they had met at the headquarters of the Guild of St. Luke before Rubens went off to Italy, and their acquaintanceship was renewed after he returned. Since Bruegel, like his younger colleague, held a commission as a court painter to the regents, it is safe to assume they saw each other in Brussels. Certainly Bruegel benefitted when the Archduke Albert permitted Rubens to live in Antwerp while retaining his court commission; the privilege having been granted to one painter, it could not be denied another.

Jan Bruegel's prestige was enormous, in part because of his illustrious family name, even though he was overshadowed by his great father and, to some extent, by his older brother. Although the public knew and appreciated the work of Pieter Bruegel the Elder, it was in artistic circles that he was revered. The most completely Flemish of all painters, he was held in an esteem by his colleagues in the Guild of St. Luke that was accorded no other men until Rubens reached his maturity.

By 1610 the two painters were close friends, in spite of the nine-year difference in their ages, and Rubens painted a portrait of Bruegel and his wife, Catherine van Marienburg. Soon thereafter the two men were working together, and for the rest of his life Bruegel used his friend's studio regardless of whether they were engaged in the same enterprise or concentrating on separate projects. Their professional relationship was always that of collaborators, even when Rubens concentrated on the central figures and Bruegel devoted himself exclusively to the landscapes, fruits, flowers, and animals that were his forte.

It did not matter to Bruegel that he was the junior partner in the firm. One of the first to recognize and appreciate Rubens' genius, he gloried in his great success. Writing to Cardinal Borromeo in 1624, less than a year before his death, Bruegel said his good friend was "fortune's favorite —to such an extent that he has received more honors and riches than any other artist of our time, and no artist in our history has more deserved them."

In 1616 or thereabouts, after Bruegel designed and built a monument to ornament his father's tomb in Brussels' Notre-Dame, he asked Rubens for a copy of his favorite painting as a decoration, and the younger man obliged by making a replica of his "Christ Giving the Keys to St. Peter" for the purpose.

In 1614 Rubens painted a portrait of Bruegel, his wife, and their two small children—a conventional, idealized work that failed to reflect his talents. Three years later Bruegel returned the compliment by painting the Rubens family, a portrait in which only Isabella Brandt comes to life.

The Bruegel family owned a house near the Rubens dwelling; this made it possible for the older man to walk to his work every morning, and he, too, formed the habit of eating only bread and cheese at noon while he continued to work. Lacking Rubens' incredible stamina and drive, however, he frequently put down his brushes for an hour to stroll through the streets of the city and clear his mind.

It was fortunate that the wives of the painters found it easy to establish a close rapport. Catherine Bruegel was more or less Isabella's age, and the two young women became inseparable, visiting each other daily. In 1615 Isabella became the godmother of one of the Bruegel daughters.

When Jan Bruegel died of the plague early in 1625, his heartbroken friend wrote his epitaph in Antwerp's Church of St. George, and later decorated his tomb with a handsome, emotionally wrought portrait. The painting subsequently disappeared and has never been located in spite of periodic, intensive searches.

The joint works of the two painters add up to an impressive list. Perhaps the most famous is their "Eve Offering Adam the Forbidden Fruit," probably painted in 1615-18, and signed by both. Only the two off-center human figures were done by Rubens; the rest of the work was Bruegel's. His style was distinctly his own, and he portrayed the many animals and plants in the painting with marvelous, delicate precision. What makes "Eve Offering Adam the Forbidden Fruit" extraordinary is the blending of Bruegel's style with that of the infinitely stronger, Baroque Rubens. The two men worked together in complete harmony.

Other painters tried to duplicate this feat but were not able to bring it off as smoothly. Rubens himself did similar work with Snyders and perhaps with Brouwer, but could not repeat the smooth flow he and Bruegel created together. In fact, he was so fond of that painting and of another painting he and Bruegel did together—"Diana"— that he kept both on display in his studio for many years, repeatedly rejecting the offers of wealthy patrons to buy them.

The seventeenth century has been called the Age of the

Artist in Europe, and never before had painters been courted, flattered, and painted so assiduously. Only in England, where dramatists and poets also were subsidized by wealthy patrons, was the artist less than the monarch of the creative world, and even there the royal family and the most powerful nobles vied with each other for the privilege of having their portraits painted by the finest artists of the day.

By 1620 or thereabouts Rubens had become so renowned and had earned so much money that it was no longer necessary for him to seek commissions, no matter what their source. When he elected to paint the portrait of a Flemish noble, banker, or merchant, he did it more as a gesture to a neighbor and friend than because he needed the work. He received so many offers to decorate churches that he could accept only a small number of these commissions, and cardinals in every nation on the Continent wrote to the Flemish bishops, asking them to use their influence in persuading Rubens to do this or that task.

Many unsolicited gifts—many of them presents from the royal families of Spain, France, and England—were sent to Rubens, who, though embarrassed by these attempts to win his favor, nevertheless accepted them. News of his collection of busts and statues had spread, and he received so many marbles and alabasters that his house was beginning to resemble a museum or gallery in the palace of a king. In a letter to Moretus, who was visiting England on business, Rubens wrote that Isabella Brandt was complaining because there was no more space to exhibit his ever-expanding collection.

At last in a position to do only the work he found interesting and challenging, Rubens made a number of attempts during the 1620's to reduce the size of his staff and cut down the enormous output of his studio. Ultimately he succeeded, to an extent, but the task was far more complicated and difficult than he had anticipated.

The ghost of Jan Rubens' scandal still haunted him, and he could never forget it or the poverty of his early years, when his mother had engaged in such gallant, frequently futile struggles. His sense of insecurity was still so great that, in spite of his intentions, he lacked the will power to turn down a commission of five hundred to one thousand gold florins, a sum far larger than any other artist of his era could command for a major work.

Certainly he knew that he could choose what he wished and that he need have no financial fears for the future, even though his expenses were high. But the fears that he himself probably could not define continued to nag him and drove him forward. He would do increasingly better work and spread his fame even more but would not give up anything he had already attained. This stand required even greater exertions of discipline, but he faced his self-imposed task with astonishing equanimity.

His relaxations were few. His daily canter beyond the city walls was a necessity imposed by his wife. Under no circumstances could Isabella Brandt be regarded as her husband's intellectual equal. Her interests were centered in her home, her children, and her friends, and although she was devoted to her husband's welfare, it is unlikely that she shared his passionate thirst for information on the international power politics of the day. It is equally unlikely that he could discuss astronomy, archaeology, chemistry, or microscope-viewing with her.

But he was one of those rare creatures, a self-sufficient man who needed no company other than his own. When he engaged in chemical experiments or studied the stars through the glass on his roof he was content. An occasional evening with old friends like Bruegel or Moretus was a pleasant but unnecessary diversion, and he preferred to spend his little free time reading or experimenting in his laboratory.

How much time he spent in the company of his children is unknown. Philip Rubens the younger makes no direct mention of the subject in the *Vita Rubenii*, Rubens himself is silent on the matter in his correspondence, and no other sources of information are available. If he treated his children as other successful men of his time dealt with theirs, they were admitted to his presence for no more than a few minutes each day. The seventeenth-century mother supervised the rearing of children, but day-to-day management was left in the hands of tutors and governesses.

What makes Peter Paul Rubens' situation intriguing is that he was typical of his time in so few ways. All that can be said with certainty is that his children showed him a far greater affection, as adults, than was customary in the period, so it well may be that he gave them greater attention and showed them more tangible signs of his love for them than did most fathers. But the evidence remains circumstantial and cannot be demonstrated.

Nothing was allowed to interfere with Rubens' work, however, and two of his greatest paintings may have been done as early as 1616. One was his monumental "Last Judgment," one of many on the subject ascribed to him, and the other was his superb "Fall of the Damned." Prince Wolfgang Wilhelm von Neuburg, Archduke of Bavaria and the Count Palatine, commissioned the "Last Judgment" for the Church of the Jesuits in Munich, and it is known to have been in place by the first months of 1618, perhaps a short time earlier. The smaller "Last Judgment" was mentioned by Rubens in a letter to Sir Dudley Carleton written in April, 1618, when he said that it had been completed by his pupils.

The major "Last Judgment" has been called Rubens' finest single painting by a number of authorities, and judged by any standards, it must be considered one of his best. It is obvious that he was influenced by the Michelangelo fresco in the Sistine Chapel, but the work is totally his own, and in it he threw off all previous conventions, Flemish as well as Roman, to become his own man and his own master.

Occupying an entire wall in the Munich Alte Pinakothek (on the other three walls of the room are displayed the smaller "Last Judgment," the "Fall of the Damned," and the "Rebel Angels," painted in 1620), the "Last Judgment" is an enormous painting that stands almost twenty feet high and is filled with human figures that mingle, writhe, face each other, and tangle. The power of the whole is awe-inspiring. Rubens must have been possessed when he painted it, and his concentrated fury is overwhelming. His coloring is brilliant, and in spite of the size of the painting, his economy of line is almost beyond belief. Perhaps Delacroix offered the best summary of the "Last Judgment" and the "Fall of the Damned" when he wrote that Rubens changed the approach of every artist to his work "by the hidden power and interior life he put into everything."

The metamorphosis of Rubens had been developing for a long time, and what makes it strange is not the fact that he made himself free of the restraints imposed on other painters, but that he should, simultaneously, continue to burden himself with more work than he could comfortably handle. There is one major difference in his approach that appeared in 1620 or thereabouts. Until that time all artists, Rubens included, were expected to deliver finished paintings that faithfully followed their sketches, and it was not unusual for a patron who was dissatisfied with a completed work to refuse payment on the grounds that it departed from the artist's approved intention.

As a consequence no artist liked to submit sketches to a client in advance, and under a polite convention that was observed by all, even Rubens, a painter, pretended that the sketch he had drawn would be used only for purposes of his own guidance. Now Rubens dispensed with the rules.

If the client insisted, he was willing to permit the man to see his sketches. If the projected work was major, he might even be persuaded to give the patron the privilege of approval, but he regarded this as no more than a formality. He reserved the right to make any changes in concept, subject matter, and style that he himself deemed appropriate, and he would be the final judge of whether he had abided by the terms of his contract. Any patron who balked at these extraordinary, one-sided terms was advised to take his commissions elsewhere, but Rubens lost no business.

No artist of any nationality had been able to obtain such powers for himself since the beginning of the Renaissance, and even Michelangelo and Raphael had been at the mercy of their patrons' whims. Rubens, the hardheaded businessman, had shrewdly judged the supply and demand that governed his work and cast off the chains that had bound Rubens, the painter. In freeing himself he had struck a blow for all artists, and after his day it was difficult for any patron to impose his ideas on an artist of stature. As Delacroix observed, Rubens single-handedly accomplished more with one blow than the Guild of St. Luke had achieved for the profession in its entire existence of more than a century.

The "Fall of the Damned," which was similar in idea and execution to the "Last Judgment," and which some authorities have seen as an extension of the same concept onto another canvas, was an added confirmation of Rubens' new stand. Having declared his independence, he refused to lean again in the direction of convention. His freedom was total, and he was free by virtue of his discipline as much as his genius. He was still the champion of Catholicism, but no authority—spiritual or temporal—would be allowed to determine the boundaries of that liberty.

It is possible that Rubens' action was sparked by an incident that began in 1612 and dragged on for the better part of a decade before the "mortal insult," as the painter called it, was rectified. In 1612 Bishop Charles Maes accepted the sketch of a painting, "The Conversion of St. Bavon," which was to grace the high altar of the Cathedral of Ghent. Other work intervened, making it impossible for Rubens to do the painting immediately, and early in 1614 the new Bishop of Ghent announced that he disliked the sketch and cancelled the contract.

Not since Rubens' youth had any patron dared to dismiss him so cavalierly, and the furious artist sent an outrageously impertinent letter to the new bishop, heaping personal scorn on him and even resorting to invective far beyond the bounds of good taste. His vanity not assuaged by this effort, Rubens also wrote a long, bitter letter of complaint to his official protector, the Archduke Albert.

If the regent replied, either soothing Rubens' vanity or castigating him for his temerity, the letter has been lost. But Albert's actions speak for themselves. A patient man, he waited until 1622, when the old bishop died and another replaced him, before doing anything.

Shortly thereafter Bishop Antoine Triest sent an order to Robert de Nole, a distinguished sculptor, to create a large, new altar for the Cathedral of Ghent, and to leave a considerable space for a triptych by Peter Paul Rubens. Bishop Triest then wrote to Rubens and, making no mention of the nine-year-old controversy, expressed the hope that the great artist would find the time to do the painting in the near future.

Bishop Triest knew precisely what he was doing. He made no mention of price, and with good reason: Had Rubens painted the triptych in 1614 he would have been paid his standard price of that period, which was five hundred gold florins. As a matter of fact, he had referred to that sum in his previous correspondence. By 1623 a Rubens triptych could not be ordered for less than one thousand florins, and a work on the scale of that required for the Cathedral of Ghent commanded fifteen hundred.

But Bishop Triest, who obviously understood the temperament of even the businessman-artist, believed that Rubens would be so delighted to win a moral victory that he would do the work for price that had first been offered to him in 1612. The bishop was right. Rubens believed he had been vindicated and painted the triptych for five hundred florins. Jan Bruegel, who paid a visit to Ghent in the autumn of 1623, delivered the finished work on his friend's behalf and received a receipt for it signed by Bishop Triest in his own hand.

The "Conversion of St. Bavon" still hangs in the place for which it was first intended, while the original, controversial sketch is on exhibition in the National Gallery, London. A comparison of the two works is instructive and amply illustrates the difference between the "old" and the "free" Rubens. The sketch is conventional, and only the genius of the artist prevents it from being trite. Since the actual triptych is bold, dramatic, and fiery in spirit, it can be argued that posterity won the real victory in the dispute.

XV By 1618, Rubens, like Alexander the Great, had conquered the known world and was anxious to extend his genius into new ventures. The "Last Judgment" and the "Fall of the Damned" are generally considered to be the last of his works in which he seemed overwhelmed by the subject of death, the last in which he shows the direct influence of Michelangelo. Thereafter he directed his newly freed talents into secular channels and, although he continued to do religious paintings, concentrated on mythological-historical subjects in which he demonstrated a hitherto hidden sense of humor.

Nowhere is his powerful and sensual Baroque style better illustrated than in his next major work, "Battle of the Amazons," now in Munich, the "Rape of the Daughters of Leucippus," in the same museum, and the tongue-in-cheek "Drunken Silenus," also in Munich. The year 1618 was one of his more productive, although Rubens wrote to Moretus late in the year that he had deliberately slowed his pace. Perhaps he believed it himself, but among his major paintings, in addition to those already mentioned, were his magnificent "Prodigal Son," now in Antwerp, "The Banishment of Hagar," the "Banquet of Achelous," and the exquisite "Virgin Presenting the Infant Jesus to St. Francis," a triptych commissioned by the Tailors' Guild for their church in Lier. The side panels are still there, and the center piece is now in Dijon.

Other major works followed in 1619, and in spite of his increasing desire to paint secular subjects the demand for religious works was so great that he did a number of them. These included two for the Church of the Jesuits in Neuberg, "The Adoration of the Shepherds" and "The Descent of the Holy Spirit." Others were the "Last Communion of St. Francis" for the Recollects' Church in Antwerp, and, for St.-Jean-de-Malines, an "Adoration of the Magi."

The *Coup de Lance,* painted in 1620, is regarded as one of the most lyrical of Rubens' religious paintings. It may be that he received no assistance in its execution, even though his studio was still filled with associates and apprentices. Perhaps he was showing sensitivity to the charge that others were doing his work for him and that he was taking the full credit, financial and otherwise.

At this same time he tried his hand at a number of hunting scenes, perhaps inspired by Jan Bruegel's success with animals. Ever competitive, Rubens could allow no other artist, even a close friend, to do better work in any field. Almost needless to say, his animals were superb, and their wild movements were typical of the great master at his best.

The "new" Rubens was also seen in his approach to portraits at this time. He accepted few private commissions, principally because sittings depended upon the convenience of the powerful lords who commissioned these works, and Rubens rightly reasoned that his own time was at least as valuable as that of his subjects. Occasionally, however, he was approached by men of such great standing that it would have been unwise to refuse them. One was Thomas Howard, Earl of Arundel and one of England's wealthiest and most active art patrons. The painting of the earl and his countess, Aletheia Talbot, dispenses with the stiff conventionality typical of most portraits and delves behind the public masks of the great, although the work can only be construed as flattering.

Shortly before painting this portrait Rubens demonstrated the skill as a diplomat that he was longing to exercise. His schedule was so filled that he had to keep Arundel waiting for several months but soothed him with a letter that, in its own way, was something of a masterpiece: "Although I have refused to paint the portraits of many princes and gentlemen of His Lordship's rank, I feel obliged to accept the honor he does me in asking for my services, for I regard him as an evangelist of art, and as the great protector of my profession."

The year 1620 is also significant because it was the year in which Rubens painted his renowned *Chapeau de Paille,* a charming portrait of an exceptionally attractive young woman wearing a pretty hat. The girl was Suzanne Fourment, the widow of one of Rubens' good friends, Raimondo del Monte; within a short time she would again be married, this time to another friend, Arnold Lunden, and again would be widowed.

Rubens and his wife were close to the whole Fourment family. Daniel, the father, was a prosperous dealer in tapestries who was one of Rubens' few intimates, and one of his sons was married to Isabella Brandt's sister Claire. In all probability no one paid much attention to the youngest of the Fourment daughters, a blue-eyed, blond child of seven years named Hélène. She was destined to play the most significant of roles in the life of Peter Paul Rubens.

As for Suzanne Fourment, the enthusiasm Rubens displayed for his subject in *Chapeau de Paille* led sharp-eyed observers of the portrait to raise their eyebrows. They may have been right when they guessed Rubens' emotional involvement, but they were premature in their judgments. He was faithful to Isabella Brandt during her lifetime, but some sources believe that, after Isabella's death, Suzanne became his mistress.

The affair was conducted discreetly, not only because of Rubens' standing as one of the first citizens of Antwerp and of Europe, but out of consideration for the dignity of the respectable Fourment family. Philip Rubens the younger glides over the subject of Suzanne in the *Vita Rubenii,* but there are several references to the girl in several of Moretus' chatty letters to his old friend. No details regarding the affair have ever been unearthed, nor is it known why Suzanne and Rubens did not marry. All that can be said with reasonable certainty is that the couple did enjoy a liaison, which was terminated when Suzanne married for the third time, her last husband being a business associate of her father's from Ghent.

The year 1620 is also important in the life of Rubens because, late in March of that year, he blithely signed his most ambitious contract. The Jesuits of Flanders were completing the construction of their new church in Antwerp, St. Charles Borromeo, and Rubens promised not only to paint thirty-nine pictures for the ceiling, altar, galleries, and side aisles, but to deliver them by the end of the year, a scant nine months later!

Included were scenes from the Old Testament as well as the New. Among them were the triumph of Queen Esther, the visit of the Queen of Sheba to King Solomon, and the sacrifice of Isaac by Abraham. Each was balanced by a New Testament scene. Two of the paintings, believed to be of St. Ignatius and St. Francis Xavier, founders of the Jesuits, were already painted, and a separate contract was made for them. The fathers agreed to pay Rubens ten thousand gold florins for the remaining thirty-seven, seven thousand of it in advance, and to give him a bonus of another five thousand florins if he completed the task on schedule. He was authorized to obtain as many collaborators as he thought he might need for this mammoth project, including Van Dyck and Bruegel, who were mentioned by name, and would supervise their work. The contract specified, however, that Rubens himself would make all of the sketches, and that he would discuss any changes with the fathers before incorporating them into his finished work.

The architects who had built the church had turned their backs on the Middle Ages and had constructed a contemporary building, which suited Rubens to perfection. Here was his opportunity to give free rein to his Baroque style, and he worked with a concentrated fury that exhausted his colleagues. It is almost anticlimactic to say that he succeeded beyond even his own expectations: the interior of the Church of St. Charles Borromeo became the Baroque wonder of the world. Soon thereafter the saying became common that Rubens had brought the Renaissance to the north, and the claim may not be exaggerated.

He not only lived up to the letter of his contract, filling the Jesuit church with masterpieces by the end of 1620, but he also found or made the time during the final months of the year to relax in work on yet another project. Sir Dudley Carleton's appetite for tapestries had become insatiable, and Rubens prepared a number of cartoons, which were then duplicated in the actual weaving of tapestries. These little gems became collectors' items and, late in the seventeenth century, became the property of such contemporary Flemish artists as Eykeus and De Wit.

Fresh from his triumph in the Jesuit church, Rubens needed another challenge, but it was difficult to find one that would match, much less surpass what he had already done. But, early in 1621, he learned of a still-secret matter that whetted his appetite anew. It may be that he heard the story from the uncommonly well-informed Moretus, although a popular legend insists that the news was passed on to him by a grateful Jesuit priest who had just come to Antwerp from France.

Whatever the source of his information, it was accurate. A magnificent new home for Marie de' Medici, widow of Henry IV and mother of Louis XIII, had just been completed in Paris by the distinguished architect, Salomon de Brosse. It was called the Palais de Luxembourg, and the Queen Mother, an art lover like so many members of her Florentine family, wanted it to be decorated in a manner that would make it the envy of the Christian world.

It was Queen Marie's intention to engage twenty or more of the world's greatest artists and to commission from each a painting. These works would be related, and each would tell a portion of the history of her late husband, already recognized as one of the greatest monarchs in the history of France. When Rubens heard of her plan, his thoughts raced, and he conceived of a project so daring that no other living artist would have had the courage to voice it: He proposed that all of the paintings be conceived and executed by one artist. There was only one man on earth capable of performing such a feat—Peter Paul Rubens.

Putting the idea into action, he hurried to Brussels to obtain the support of the regents and found them exceptionally amenable for reasons of their own. Their relations with Spain were increasingly strained, and they would be far stronger if they obtained the support of another major power. The logical choice was France, the southern neighbor of the Low Countries, and no man was better suited for the delicate task of arranging the liaison than Rubens. The Archduchess Isabella is generally credited with the idea of giving Rubens this diplomatic assignment.

In view of Rubens' own desire to become a diplomat, however, it is far more likely that the scheme originated with him and that he, in turn, convinced the archduchess he was the right man for the job. If he could win the confidence of the real rulers of France—the Queen Mother and her adviser, Armand Cardinal Richelieu—during the course of his work on the paintings, when he would be in contact with them from time to time, it would be a relatively easy matter for him to arrange a closer relationship between the courts of Brussels and Paris.

Once the matter was approved, the regents wasted no time. Their ambassador to the court of France, Baron de Vicq, was called home for instructions. On his return to France he found himself blocked by the continuing feud between Louis XIII and his mother, who were not on speaking terms at the moment. But the subtle intervention of Cardinal Richelieu, who himself was admitted to a place on the king's council and almost overnight became the First Minister of France, was responsible for a reconciliation early in November.

Baron de Vicq, who kept himself informed of such developments, called on the Queen Mother the next day to inform her that his own royal master and mistress were happy to offer her the services of their own court painter, the incomparable Peter Paul Rubens, to carry out the large project she had in mind. He reported that Marie was too startled to reply.

The baron next called on Cardinal Richelieu, and it was no accident that he had himself just received a glowing letter from the Jesuits of Antwerp, in which they told him in detail of the art wonders Rubens had created for them. The cunning Richelieu knew at once that more was at stake than the decoration of a palace, and he played his usual game. If he could persuade Her Majesty to listen to him, he told the ambassador, perhaps the artist Rubens would not object to paying a visit to Paris for the purpose of discussing the matter of the paintings.

Baron de Vicq already knew Rubens' answer but was obliged to observe the amenities. He wrote to the regents, and they, in turn, asked Rubens whether he would be willing to make the journey. The budding diplomat wrote a marvelous reply, indicating that his days were unbelievably crowded and that he was working from sunrise to sunset on projects that could not wait. But he professed himself so overwhelmed by the prospect of renewing his acquaintance with Marie de' Medici, whom, he was careful to point out, he had met in their mutual youth at her proxy wedding to Henry IV, that he gladly would drop everything else.

Queen Marie was duly flattered and agreed to invite the painter to visit her. Louis XIII sulked as he always did when he was not the center of attention, but his mother and Cardinal Richelieu soothed him, and he granted his royal permission for the visit.

Rubens had no intention of traveling like an ordinary portrait painter in search of work, and he made careful preparations for his journey, but acted with deliberate haste. He arranged with the regents for a young nobleman at the Brussels court, Robert de Viles, to accompany him as a secretary, and the mere fact that a prominent blueblood would condescend to act in that capacity on the staff of a mere artist was certain to impress Marie and the cardinal.

Then, working with his usual frenzied speed, Rubens designed a coat of arms for himself, and although he was not entitled to one, an assistant painted it in gold on the doors of his luxurious carriage, which was usually used by Isabella and the children when they went out for drives in the countryside. He also designed a "Rubens household livery," and a tailor obligingly worked day and night to make uniforms for a coachman, his assistant, and a valet, all three of whom also were members of the party.

Since none of the horses in the Rubens stable were sufficiently impressive, the painter also paid a small fortune for

163

a matched team of six massive geldings. Then, with the carriage also freshly painted and its interior refurbished, he set out on his journey.

Escorted by his servants, he paused in Brussels long enough for a final conference with the regents, who gave him a number of expensive gifts for the Queen Mother, King Louis, and Cardinal Richelieu. It was obvious this was no ordinary journey of an artist who was going to Paris for work. Then, with Robert de Viles added to the party, Rubens set out on the cobbled road to France.

It was common knowledge that the movements of foreigners and their mode of travel were reported to Paris, where visitors were judged accordingly by the crafty Richelieu. Rubens and De Viles took suites at the best inns, distributed largesse like great lords, and ordered sumptuous repasts, even though the artist left the rich dishes and heavy wines untouched. Unknown even to the regents, he had already refined his original plan and was prepared to outline a scheme to Marie de' Medici that was far bolder than anyone else realized.

XVI The Renaissance had come to France somewhat later than it had to the Italian states and the Low Countries, but the nation that was emerging as the wealthiest and most powerful on the Continent was making up for lost time in the seventeenth century. Henry IV had not only ended the costly religious civil wars, but his encouragement of industry, agriculture, foreign trade, and exploration were creating a new France. Nowhere was his farsighted planning more evident than in Paris, whose population of more than one million made it the largest metropolitan center in Europe. Henry's building program—which he had inaugurated with the construction of the Palais Royal, the Pont Neuf, the Ministry of Justice, and the expansion of the Louvre—was still in progress more than a decade after his death. Certainly the proud claim of Parisians that they lived in the world's loveliest city was not lacking in foundation.

Peter Paul Rubens, like the countless artists who have visited Paris through the centuries after his time, was dazzled by the place. His previous travels had caused him to think of himself as cosmopolitan, and to an extent his attitude was justified, but nothing had prepared him for the stunning architecture, the charm, and the sophistication of the French capital. Moving into the house of Baron de Vicq, he reacted like any other tourist, and while awaiting a summons by the Queen Mother, he spent his days sightseeing.

Marie de' Medici had her own way of dealing with people, and she let him wait. Rubens arrived in Paris early in December, 1621, but he was not granted a royal audience for a month. During that time he held one brief meeting with Cardinal Richelieu, who obviously wanted to form his own estimate of the Fleming, but nothing of consequence was decided at this session.

Rubens did not waste his time, however; he already knew a great deal about the basic situation of the French royal family, and he learned more. It was no secret that the Queen Mother was a greedy, vain woman, and the fact that she wanted to honor her late husband was an irony that could not have been lost on Rubens.

King Henry's romantic first marriage had ended in an annulment some years after he had discovered his wife had been unfaithful to him and had banished her to a remote fortress. There had been no lack of women in his life, however, and his record had been unique: fifty-six known women had been his mistresses. The fifty-fifth, Gabrielle d'Estrées, had been responsible for his nominal conversion to Catholicism, and shortly after her unfortunate death, at a time when he had been contemplating marriage to her, he had contracted a marriage of political convenience to the Florentine princess.

There had been no love lost between the dynamic, farseeing Henry and his self-aggrandizing, ultraconservative second wife. He had done his duty by siring her son, who was now Louis XIII, but in the main his relationship with her had been formal and remote, and it was said that she had not wept when he was assassinated at the climax of a plot in which his fifty-sixth mistress had been involved.

For more than ten years Marie de' Medici had done her utmost to reverse the tide of history and undo all that her husband had accomplished. She had been checked in her designs by the country's great nobles in a running feud that had resulted in her estrangement from her son, and although she did not yet realize it, she would be further thwarted when Richelieu, whom she trusted implicitly, consolidated King Henry's gains and led the nation to still higher plateaus.

Rubens, who loved beauty, must have shuddered when he was admitted to the Queen Mother's presence. She had been a plain girl when he had seen her almost two decades earlier, and her magnificent gowns and jewels could not hide the fact that she had become one of the homeliest women in Europe.

But the Fleming demonstrated his talents as a diplomat by charming Marie, and among the gifts he presented to her were two small paintings he had done expressly for her since his arrival in Paris. When it became evident that she was enjoying his company and that he had made an impression on her, he told her his idea: Before reducing the history of Henry IV to canvas, he proposed that he paint a series of pictures on the subject of the Queen Mother herself.

His touch was unerring, and he had played precisely the right chord. Marie found the idea irresistible and immediately contracted for twenty-four paintings to be displayed in her Palais de Luxembourg. Rubens, always the shrewd man of business, would receive the staggering sum of twenty-five thousand gold ecus for the task, by far the largest commission ever given to any member of his profession.

In spite of the homeliness of his subject, whom he flattered with great subtlety, he carried out the assignment with enormous success, and his works are still on exhibition. He worked with almost blinding speed; never had he produced paintings so extravagantly Baroque, so powerful, and so harmonious. All of the paintings were masterpieces and rank among the world's most precious art treasures.

Not only was Queen Marie delighted, perhaps overwhelmed, but she spent many hours posing for the artist, and during this time Rubens succeeded in winning her complete confidence. He arranged for a much closer liaison between the court of the Queen Mother and that of the regents in Brussels, and he set up a line of communication between Marie and the Archduke Albert that was a factor in the establishment of close relations between France and Belgium that would endure for centuries. Rubens cannot be given credit for this rapprochement, to be sure, but he was instrumental in creating the machinery that made the exchange of diplomatic confidences possible.

His initial effort in his second profession was a triumph that exceeded even his own high hopes. It was all the more remarkable because he managed to conceal his true opinion of France and the French. For reasons he never explained to anyone, he entertained a lifelong dislike of France, a fact which he admitted on rare occasions and in guarded terms when corresponding with Moretus and Nicolas Peiresc, the French intellectual who became one of his few close friends. He knew the diplomat's art of simulation and revealed nothing of his true feelings to Queen Marie. Even more important, his emotions were in no way reflected in the superb Marie de' Medici series.

During one of Rubens' sojourns in Paris a new international crisis erupted, and his services were required to help smooth the ruffled waters. The twelve-year truce that had enabled nominally Spanish Belgium and Flanders to live in peace with the independent Netherlands came to an end, and Philip IV of Spain was demanding terms that Prince Maurice of Nassau found unacceptable. A new war threatened to decimate the Low Countries, and at this critical juncture the Archduke Albert died.

The Archduchess Isabella, who had always been the more forceful of the regents, immediately sent a letter to Rubens, asking him to do everything possible to persuade Paris to mediate in the troubles between Madrid and The Hague. He realized that the Queen Mother had no real voice in the affairs of France, but that Richelieu humored her because he was using her as a stepping-stone to achieve total mastery of the nation himself.

So he utilized the services of Marie, who recommended to the cardinal that France enter negotiations with both parties. But Rubens remained a realist, and, in a blunt letter to the Archduchess Isabella, he warned that the "newcomers in Madrid"—meaning Philip IV and his ministers—were belligerent men who would try to strike a hard bargain with the Dutch.

What the artist-diplomat failed to realize was that Cardinal Richelieu had ideas of his own on the matter, and that, after he consolidated his own hold on the reins of government, he would conclude an alliance with the Protestant Netherlands for the purpose of curbing the powers of Catholic Spain. What Rubens also did not know was that the cardinal planned to use his own efforts as an artist to solidify the reconciliation of Louis XIII with his mother. Perhaps Marie had conveniently "forgotten" the plan to memorialize the life of Henry IV in a series of paintings, but Richelieu, who knew the king worshiped his late father, had a tenacious memory.

For a period of several years Rubens almost literally commuted between Antwerp and Paris, and, as usual, he worked on a large number of other projects during this time. He delivered the first nine of his paintings of the Marie de' Medici series to the Queen Mother in the spring of 1623, and he completed the last of them late in 1624. In May of 1625 year the Princess Henrietta Maria, daughter of Henry IV and Marie de' Medici, was married to King

Charles I of England, and the paintings were unveiled during the premarital festivities. Rubens was a guest of honor at the Luxembourg on that occasion, a rare honor for a painter, who ordinarily would have been required by the demands of protocol to remain in the background, no matter how great his talents.

The paintings remained in their original settings until modern times. Then, in order to make them available to the largest possible audience, they were moved to what had been the great Hall of State in the Louvre, where they are currently on exhibition.

The paintings served Richelieu's purpose, although it was necessary for Rubens to distort history somewhat and to forget the feud between Marie de' Medici and her son that had led France to the brink of civil war and, for a time, had caused the Queen Mother to be banished from Paris. The extraordinary paintings created a new sensation that made the artist the talk of France and caused the great English nobles who were in Paris for the wedding to inundate the artist with requests for portraits.

In a letter to Peiresc, Rubens said that Marie de' Medici "has expressed her great joy on many occasions, and has repeated her words to anyone within hearing. The King has done me the honor of visiting the gallery himself, and showed himself very pleased."

The Abbé de St.-Ambroise, who was recognized as a leading French art critic in the seventeenth century, delivered a verdict that was a summation of his nation's attitude, and Peiresc lost no time in communicating his views to Rubens:

> No one else in all of Europe could have brought such a vast work to a successful conclusion. The Italians would take more than ten years to do what you have done in four, and would not even dream of supplying

pictures of such dimensions. The Abbé declares that you are unique, that you stand high above every other artist now alive in the world, and that your paintings of Marie de Medicis will be immortal.

Three Flemish painters were known to be working as Rubens' assistants at the time, Guillaume Panneels, Justus van Egmont, and Jacob Moermans, who is known to posterity only because he was responsible, under the terms of Rubens' will, for selling those paintings still in the master's studio after his death. All three were journeymen of no particular talent, men who were capable of filling in backgrounds for Rubens' ordinary portrait work, but good for little else. All probably worked with him on the Marie de' Medici series.

With this tremendous project finished, Rubens was ready to begin work on the even more ambitious project, the Henry IV series. He signed a contract, which was witnessed by no less a personage than Cardinal Richelieu, in which he promised "to paint and present all the battles of King Henry the Great, his encounters, combats, captures and sieges of towns; together with the triumphs of the said victories after the manner of the triumphs of the Romans, and following the schema to be provided by Her Majesty."

As he had done in preparing the previous series, he first made monochrome sketches, which he submitted for the approval of the Queen Mother, the cardinal, and, in this instance, King Louis. All at once, however, there were unexplained delays, which Marie vaguely indicated were caused by the fact that the gallery in the Palais du Luxembourg in which they were to be exhibited was not yet finished; hence the size of the paintings could not be determined. But Rubens consulted with Salomon de Brosse, the architect, who assured him that the gallery was finished and actually showed it to him.

It became evident that Marie de' Medici was in no great hurry to glorify her late husband. She herself was the talk of cultured Europe after suffering years of relative obscurity, and she wanted nothing to dim the luster of her new image. Only a few days after the wedding of the princess to Charles I, Rubens wrote to Peiresc:

> I have the feeling that there will be great difficulties over the subjects of the other gallery. They should, notwithstanding this, be easy to carry out, without any untoward incident. The theme is rich and abundant enough to fill two galleries; but the Cardinal de Richelieu, although I have submitted a written scheme to him in detail, is so busy with affairs of state that he has not had the time to glance at it. What may occupy the time of Her Majesty I do not know, but she also informs me that she has not yet had the opportunity to study my plan.

Deciding it would be a mistake in tactics for a man of his stature to be kept waiting indefinitely, hat in hand, Rubens decided to return to Antwerp as soon as he received his final payment for the first series. Thereafter he would come to Paris when summoned.

The Queen Mother was a Medici in every sense of word, and all members of her family, including Lorenzo the Great, had been known as bargain hunters. Notwithstanding the fact that Rubens had a written contract, she haggled with him and tried to pay him less than he was owed. He stood his ground, however, and it appears that he treated her as an equal and exchanged sharp words with her. Rubens was annoyed and confided to Peiresc, "It is possible that if they do not show the same punctiliousness in paying me as I put into the service of the Queen Mother, I shall not easily be persuaded to return."

He had been promised the even larger fee of thirty-six

thousand gold écus for the new series but knew the contract would be worthless if the Queen Mother went back on her written word regarding the first. Apparently he toyed with the idea of removing the paintings from the Palais du Luxembourg and taking them back to Antwerp with him, but common sense prevailed and he refrained from taking such a drastic step. High-strung kings and queens had been known to go to war when subjected to personal insults.

The situation was galling, although Rubens did not actually need the money, and other matters required his presence in the Low Countries, where fighting had been renewed between the Netherlands and Spain. No one sought peace more fervently than did the Archduchess Isabella, and no one worked harder toward that end than Peter Paul Rubens.

He himself had become one of the principal negotiators and was slowly hammering out the terms of a new treaty, working with representatives of Maurice of Nassau, the archduchess, and Philip IV. The end results he wanted were still a distant goal, but on June 5, 1625, he received a personal reward that changed his status. King Philip sent him a certificate and patents of ennoblement, and the Archduchess Isabella added her own touch by appointing him a gentleman of her household. From that time forward Rubens was entitled to call himself Don Peter Paul, to carry a sword, and to use the crest he had already designed and had emblazoned on his carriage four years before.

Returning to Antwerp by way of Brussels, the new nobleman paused long enough at the regent's court to paint his finest portrait of Isabella, now in the Pitti Palace, and also to paint a visiting monarch, King Vladislav Sigismund of Poland. While in France he had painted Louis XIII and had been paid promptly; he had also painted several prominent members of the court, and was by no stretch of the imagination suffering because of the Queen Mother's tardiness in paying him what she owed him.

Her reluctance was not based exclusively on monetary considerations, at least insofar as Cardinal Richelieu was concerned. The marriage of the princess to King Charles had made France the ally of England, and a secret alliance had been worked out with England's good friend, the Netherlands. Therefore France was on the threshold of war with Spain, and the cardinal did not enjoy the prospect of giving new working and living quarters in the royal palace, the Louvre, to an artist-diplomat who had just been ennobled by Spain.

Regardless of the turn the negotiations for the new French contract might take, Rubens was pleased. His Marie de' Medici series had made him one of Europe's most famous men, and he had won a place in the Spanish nobility, thanks to his services as a diplomat. But the painter's appetite was whetted, and he sought still greater glories.

XVII Rubens the painter and Rubens the diplomat constantly helped and supported each other. Perhaps the best example can be found just prior to Rubens' return to Antwerp from Paris after the wedding of the princess to Charles I. The most prominent member of the English party in France was the Duke of Buckingham, the king's favorite and, for all practical purposes, his principal minister of state, a man who was sometimes said to rule in all but name.

Rubens painted two portraits of the duke: one, a standard work, is now in the Pitti Palace; the second, a figure on horseback, was destroyed by fire in 1940. For the first Rubens received silver plate worth two thousand gold crowns, and for the second he was paid three thousand crowns in cash, both of them princely sums worthy of Buckingham. Of far greater importance, however, is the fact that during the sittings in the Paris home of the British ambassador, the painter and his subject held intensive discussions on the subject of European politics. London was on the verge of terminating the betrothal of the sister of Philip IV to the cousin of King Charles, at that time the heir to the British throne, and Rubens heard the news before it reached Madrid. This enabled him to pass it along to the Archduchess Isabella. Rubens and Buckingham also explored various possible peace formulas, and although nothing concrete developed, each gained a greater appreciation of the other. Certainly Buckingham found out that Rubens was a strong potential ally, a man who valued peace in the Low Countries more than he did the cause of Spain.

There is also an amusing sidelight to these talks that involve the third Peter Paul Rubens, the businessman. Since Buckingham was a collector of antiques and Rubens' marbles were renowned, Buckingham wanted them. Rubens was reluctant to part with his possessions but was always willing to entertain a bid, provided it was high enough; he bargained pleasantly with the duke when conversation on other subjects lagged. It is no wonder that Buckingham later called the artist "the most brilliant of men I have ever met."

At no time was Rubens idle. It might be noted that in 1624, while working on the French project, he also painted a great "Adoration of the Magi" for the high altar of St. Michael in Antwerp, a work now in Antwerp's Royal Museum.

By the mid-1620's the art collection amassed by the great painter was one of the finest in Europe. His own taste impeccable, he had acquired works that gave his private gallery a standing higher than that of many wealthy monarchs. Among his paintings were works by Titian, Correggio, Tintoretto, Van Eyck, Van Dyck, Holbein, and Bronzino. He owned eighteen paintings by Brouwer, twelve by Jan Bruegel, and a number of canvases by others who had worked with him, as well as drawings by Veronese, Titian, Tintoretto, and Dürer.

Because of his travels he had little time to enjoy his collection, which was entrusted to the care of his wife. He painted two portraits of Isabella Brandt during this period, one now in the Uffizi Gallery and the better known in the Cleveland Museum of Art. She was in her thirties, and the changes in her appearance were marked. She was still a pretty woman, although she had gained a great deal of weight and had aged considerably, but the chief difference was in her eyes. Life as the spouse of one of the most celebrated and successful men of the age had made her long-suffering and patient.

There was no hint in her appearance of her illness, probably tuberculosis, which she had managed to conceal from her husband. By the final months of 1625 her condition worsened, however, and the physicians Rubens summoned confined her to her bed. Nothing could be done for her, and she continued to decline.

Rubens, now at the zenith of his career at the age of forty-nine, could do nothing for her. Abandoning all attempts to work, he spent his days at her bedside, nursing her himself and trying to will her to improve. His care and efforts were futile, however, and on June 20, 1626, Isabella Brandt Rubens died at the age of thirty-five.

Rubens was crushed and bewildered by her passing, and Moretus comments that he was "a lost soul."

Isabella Brandt had participated in none of her husband's triumphs, remaining in the background while he consorted with the great and powerful. But she had been his anchor, and the widower, his house filled with children, was so bewildered that, after receiving the condolences of his friends, he locked himself in his house and saw no one. Not even in his time of grief was Rubens willing to allow others to become aware of his vulnerability. A letter he wrote to his friend, Pierre Dupuy, less than a month after Isabella Brandt's death contains his only known comments on her passing and the effect of her death on him:

As for myself, I have lost my most intimate companion, whom I could and must in reason always love; for she had none of the faults of her sex. She was neither morose-tempered nor weak; but so kind, so good and so filled with all womanly virtues that everyone loved her during her life and mourns her since her death. Such a loss touches my inmost being; and since the only cure for all our ills is forgetfulness, child of time, I must needs await from him my only comfort. But it will be hard for me to disentangle my sorrow from the memory I shall hold all my life of this dear and adored soul.

I believe that travel would help me, for it would tear me away from the sight of all that surrounds me, and at length revive me from my misery.

Having raised one corner of the curtain that separated the inner Peter Paul Rubens from the world, the artist lowered it again. In none of his correspondence thereafter did he mention his late wife's name or his own sorrow. He discussed business matters and international politics at length, but his pride in the image he had created from his youth would not permit him to reveal to the world that he was suffering in a lonely vacuum.

Philip Rubens the younger mentions the death of Isabella Brandt very briefly in the *Vita Rubenii.* The whole family mourned this best of all women, he declares, and Rubens himself drew even closer to the children, consoling them as best he could. The biographer provides no details.

In the summer and autumn of 1626 Rubens did no work, but by November he roused himself sufficiently from his lethargy to take his own advice, and he went off to Paris, where he remained for three weeks, visiting with some of the friends he had made there. During his sojourn Cardinal Richelieu summoned him for a conference, which was held at the First Minister's home rather than his office. A secretary recorded that the two men were closeted for "about two hours," but no details of the meeting have been made known.

A month or two earlier Rubens had concluded his agreement to sell a number of paintings in his collection to the Duke of Buckingham, and he traveled to Calais, where he personally crated the art works and stored them in the hold of a Royal Navy barque-of-war for transfer to England. He left no permanent record of the paintings involved in the sale, other than to comment in a letter to Buckingham that, "as agreed," he was including four works of his own. The wealthy duke paid him fifty thousand gold sovereigns for the collection, and Rubens was now so wealthy that he enjoyed complete financial independence for the rest of his life.

The weather in Calais at the end of November was miserable. Rain fell steadily day after day, a cold wind whipped in from the English Channel, and Rubens was forced to take to his bed with the first serious illness he had ever suffered. As in all personal matters, he refused to discuss his physical condition with anyone but his physicians, and no one, down to the present day, has ever learned the precise nature of his disability. The few guarded remarks in his correspondence and the somewhat less cryptic references made by close friends in their letters to him make it seem likely that he suffered a severe attack of rheumatism. In any event the ailment was chronic and grew much worse during the final fourteen years of his life. Some medical-literary detectives have concluded that he was suffering from recurring attacks of gout, but the question is one of many in the life of Rubens that has never been resolved.

All that can be said for certain is that he spent two weeks in bed in his Calais lodgings, and that, when he left the port town for Brussels, he was obliged to walk with the assistance of a cane. Thereafter he frequently carried a walking stick, and in his final years it was his constant companion.

Certainly it is no exaggeration to say that Rubens lost his youth when Isabella Brandt died. The self-portraits he painted in his last decade and a half reveal a man who continued to dress well, but who aged rapidly. He gained considerable weight, the jowls beneath his full, graying beard were heavy, and deep, permanent smudges appeared under his eyes.

By January, 1627, Rubens was back in Antwerp, exhausted after his travels but ready to embark on a new scheme to earn large sums of money. For more than a decade he had experimented with the art of engraving, hoping to make inexpensive copies of his paintings. For several years he had worked with a neighbor and friend, the Dutch Lucas Vorsterman, who is generally believed to have made the best reproductions in copper of the master's works. But the two men had quarreled over some trifling matter, and Vorsterman had gone off to England. He would return to Flanders in 1630, but thereafter he would work exclusively with Van Dyck, never resuming his relationship with his former friend.

Rubens hired several engravers in succession but was such a perfectionist that none of them satisfied him. Finally, at the suggestion of Moretus, he worked with Christopher Jegher, who was unique among Antwerp's engravers because he worked in wood rather than metal. The pair were associated for a number of years.

Not yet ready to return to serious painting, Rubens designed a large bowl for King Charles I of England which was executed by a silversmith. Word of this work spread quickly, and there were so many requests from wealthy nobles for Rubens-inspired artifacts that the painter obliged by making a number of other designs for bowls and cups that were then fashioned of either gold or silver. He also drew a number of sketches for small ivory statuettes, which he then turned over to sculptors who were moving into this increasingly lucrative field of endeavor.

It is almost certain that Rubens and Suzanne Fourment became involved in their affair at some time during the winter of 1627 and that the relationship lasted for about a year. Then Suzanne met the man who became her last husband, and after terminating her liaison with Rubens she married and went off to Brussels.

Rubens' correspondence with Peiresc and Dupuy at this time reveals the artist's growing concern with the increasingly repressive measures taken by the Church in Flanders to command the loyalty of the people. The Counter-Reformation was at the height of its power and influence, and the death of the Archduke Albert had removed a liberalizing force. Several of the older bishops, themselves humanists, had died in recent years, and their successors were archconservatives who combined forces with other reactionary elements in the Flemish Church.

They promulgated new rules that promptly drove some of Flanders' most talented men across the border into Holland, which promptly benefitted from their labors and became the intellectual capital of Western Europe. Protestants and Jews were forbidden to worship in public and were subject to expulsion from the country unless they accepted conversion to Catholicism. In addition, the Church confiscated and took possession of their property. Catholics were not spared the zealous concern of the bishops either. Any man who failed to attend mass for two Sundays out of three was automatically excommunicated, which meant that he had to flee into penniless exile.

Peter Paul Rubens remained devout in his own faith, but he deplored the "new morality," which outlawed such Flemish institutions as gambling and prostitution, both of which were driven underground. He is known to have refused to take part in the dreary religious processions

181

which had taken the place of the festivals that had made Antwerp one of the most colorful cities on the Continent, and in which all citizens were expected to participate.

Rubens despised the policies that sent so many of his friends out of the country. "I think of myself as a citizen of the world," he said in a letter to Peiresc. "More than all else I long for peace on earth, and am willing to devote all of my time and labors to that end. But I fear that the policies now afflicting us will not bring peace."

He found his own way to protest. The authorities could have compelled him to march in the religious processions but would have made themselves ridiculous if they had dragged him through the streets in chains. Neither they nor he forgot that he was the greatest of living artists, a man ennobled by Spain. From Rubens' standpoint his absence from the processions was a negative form of protest; the people would not notice his failure to participate, so his protest would remain a secret.

In his work he had total freedom. His nudes, glorifying the Flemish woman, were marvelously frank studies, free of any hint of sly eroticism, and he fully intended to continue to present them in both his religious and secular paintings, making no distinction between the two.

Rubens' nudes appeared in many of his more celebrated religious works which already decorated the finest churches of Flanders and other countries. Superb nudes appeared in secular works, including paintings owned by Philip IV of Spain, the Defender of the Church, as well as in the panels done on commission for Her Catholic Majesty, the Queen Mother of France.

Rubens did as he pleased, making his own rules and obeying no others. It is important, however, to understand his rebellion in the light of what he himself believed. He remained committed to Catholicism, and in both his painting and his diplomatic work he thought of himself as a defender of the faith. But he made a sharp distinction between the teachings of the Church and the overzealous attitude adopted by the Flemish bishops. He chose to work for the betterment of mankind and the salvation of souls from within the Church, but that did not stop him from opposing the repressive measures that, as he and every other intelligent Fleming could see, were causing the people to become increasingly lethargic in the practice of their own devotions.

It is known that Rubens carried out a vitally important diplomatic mission in 1628 that further demonstrates his independence. In the spring of the preceding year France and Spain had signed a treaty that had isolated England, and King Philip IV had made no secret of the fact that he hoped to conduct a holy war that would force London to accept Catholicism as England's official religion.

The Duke of Buckingham sent a secret emissary to Antwerp and asked Rubens to propose an armistice with Spain and a free trade treaty that would include England, Spain, Denmark, the Netherlands, and Flanders. Rubens immediately went to Madrid to lay the proposal before the Archduchess Isabella, who decided England was asking too much. But she used her influence in Madrid, and the result was a new peace treaty between England and Spain, Philip IV realizing he could not make war on England without the cooperation of Brussels and Antwerp. So Rubens played a diplomatic role in moves that assured peace—at the expense of the projected crusade to return England forcibly to the Catholic fold.

Almost simultaneously, however, the artist threw himself with renewed vigor into work that would strengthen the Church against heresy. He happily accepted a commission from the archduchess to do eighteen tapestry cartoons for the Convent of Discalced Carmelites in Madrid. These tapestries, which still hang in the place for which they were woven, were called the "Triumph of the Eucharist," and firmly support the Catholic dogma of the Real Presence, one of the Church's major theological disagreements with the Protestants.

A man of high, unwavering principle, Rubens acted in accordance with his own beliefs, and his consistency in the face of determined opposition within the Church soon won him greater triumphs than any of his previous achievements.

XVIII   The preparation of the "Triumph of the Eucharist"
marked Rubens' return to a
regular schedule of work, and
he labored without interruption until the early summer of
1628, when he received a letter from the Duke of Olivarez,
the First Minister of Spain, requesting his appearance
before Philip IV and asking him to bring copies of all of his
diplomatic correspondence. Moretus and other friends
were afraid the artist would get into trouble because he had
been acting contrary to Spanish policy, but Rubens dis-
agreed. He wrote to Peiresc that he saw an opportunity to
convert the king and court to his own point of view, an
egotistical approach that reveals his supreme self-confidence.

Late in August or early in September, while he was on the
road, Rubens heard the shocking news that the Duke of
Buckingham had been assassinated. The English believed
the killer had been in the pay of Spain, and the peace of
Western Europe again was threatened, even though the
charge was false. The atmosphere at the court in Madrid
was tense when the Fleming presented himself to the king.

It was assumed in London, Paris, and other cities that Rubens was placed on trial in Madrid, but this allegation was untrue. Philip IV, Olivarez, and several others interrogated him at length and studied his correspondence, but these were informal sessions that in no way resembled a trial or hearing. Rubens appears to have conducted himself with vigorous self-assurance and lived up to his prediction, writing to Peiresc that the king and First Minister had adopted his suggestions and would work, henceforth, to ensure the maintenance of peace.

His letter also revealed other, even better news. Rubens was now the official guest of the crown, living quarters and a studio having been made available to him in the royal palace. He had been commissioned to paint the portraits of Philip and other members of the royal family. In all, Rubens painted five portraits of the monarch, one of them an equestrian figure. That which was subsequently judged the best was destroyed a century later in a fire; of the others, one is now in the Kunsthaus, Zurich, and another hangs in the Kunsthistorisches Museum, Vienna.

Queen Elizabeth, a member of the house of Bourbon, hated sitting for her portrait, but Rubens managed to persuade her to sit for one painting. While in Madrid he also painted interpretations of the works of other painters whom he admired, among them Titian, Raphael, and Tintoretto. These included various portraits: the Duke of Alba, the Emperor Charles V, the Emperor Ferdinand, Ippolito Cardinal de' Medici, and a number of others; he also did an "Adam and Eve in Paradise" and an "Adonis and Venus." In all, not including the portraits of the royal family, he painted twenty-one works while in Madrid, and all of them were exhibited in the royal palace.

Perhaps the most significant aspect of his Spanish sojourn was the formation of a new friendship with a young Spanish artist, the only association of its kind that he formed there.

Diego Velásquez, the son-in-law and former pupil of Francisco Pacheco, long the court painter, also held an appointment at the court. At twenty-nine years old, he was somber, quiet, and industrious, and although his work showed promise of the greatness that he would display in the future, he was simple and almost timid in his approach to painting.

Rubens became friendly with the younger man, his personality for a time threatening to swamp the quiet Spaniard, who was awed by his friend's talent and renown. Rubens is rightly credited with playing an important role in Velásquez's development, first by praising the direct simplicity of his work, and then by successfully urging him to study the great painters of the past in Rome.

According to a contemporary account that is accepted as valid, Rubens and Velásquez spent an entire day together at the Escorial, the royal retreat a few miles from Madrid, studying the paintings of various masters in the palace, with Rubens explaining various techniques, then comparing Velásquez's work favorably with the painting under examination. By the end of the day Velásquez was filled with a desire to emulate the work of his friend and had accepted his urgent advice to live and work in Italy.

Certainly the later work of Velásquez indicated his indebtedness to Rubens. Some historians have hunted for hidden motives in Rubens, seeking complex reasons for his generosity to the younger painter, but they have missed something essential in Rubens' character. He knew that his own immortality was assured and, feeling no jealousy of any of his contemporaries, was quick to recognize talent in others. Velásquez was regarded as an ordinary painter at the Spanish court, and even his father-in-law, who praised his sobriety, regarded his work as run-of-the-mill. But Rubens was aware of the young Spaniard's genius, just as he had been in the case of Van Dyck, and used his own enormous prestige to kindle the other's ambition.

Rubens remained in Madrid until late April, 1629, during which time France and England concluded a new peace that both nations hoped would be lasting. Throughout his Spanish sojourn Rubens spent most of his free time with Velásquez, who called him master; whether they corresponded until the end of Rubens' life is possible, but not certain. It is posterity's misfortune that most of these exchanges between two of the world's greatest artists have been lost—assuming there really were such letters. From time to time various letters purportedly part of that correspondence have appeared, but without exception they are believed to be forgeries. What matters is that Rubens' encouragement and advice helped Velásquez to live up to his own dazzling potential.

Rubens returned to Flanders in May, 1629, far wealthier than he had been prior to his departure; Philip IV had given him many gifts of cash, a set of gold plate worth a royal ransom, and a sword with a jeweled scabbard and hilt that was also worth a fortune. Rubens received yet another gift that was worth even more to him: Pending the appointment of a permanent new ambassador to England, Rubens was being sent to London as the official ambassador of Spain. This was the highest appointment in the diplomatic service that he had ever received, and it confirmed his professional standing as a statesman. Not even Rubens himself could have asked for more.

Rubens arrived in London on June 5, after a stay at home of only two weeks, and presented his credentials to King Charles I at Greenwich, where the court had gone for the summer. The Fleming immediately found himself in a precarious diplomatic situation. Chateauneuf, the new French ambassador, was following the instructions of the wily Richelieu and was attempting to keep England and Spain at arm's length from each other. Rubens hoped to persuade the English to sign a new treaty of friendship with

Madrid, but Chateauneuf thwarted him at every turn. King Charles actually preferred the friendship of France to that of Spain, and he used the continuing absence of the permanent Spanish envoy as an excuse to procrastinate. To summarize Rubens' accomplishments as a diplomat during his stay in England: He achieved little, and the damp climate was responsible for attacks of rheumatism that crippled him and caused him to long for the day when he could go home.

Of far greater importance than his diplomatic achievements is his activity as a painter in England. At the king's personal request he painted the portraits of Charles and Queen Henrietta Maria. He was also commissioned by the crown to paint an "Allegory of Peace and War" and another large work, "St. George and the Dragon." He painted another portrait of his old friend, the Earl of Arundel, and may have done still another. One of the most unusual of his portraits was "Old Parr," his subject being a man purportedly almost one hundred and fifty years of age.

Rubens' relief was infinite when the new Spanish ambassador, Don Carlos Coloma, finally arrived in England early in January, 1630, but Rubens was instructed by the Duke of Olivarez to remain at his post until the new treaty of friendship was signed. Curbing his impatience, the artist-diplomat stayed in London until April.

When he finally departed, he went home laden with gifts from Charles I as valuable as those Philip of Spain had given him, and he was said to be one of the wealthiest men in Europe. A final gift from Charles surprised and delighted him. In a farewell ceremony he was made a baronet and henceforth was entitled to call himself Sir Peter Paul, a title his elder son would inherit. He had now enjoyed the distinction of being a patrician in both England and Spain.

Returning to Antwerp in mid-April, 1630, Rubens immediately brought pressure to bear on France, hoping he would receive his long-delayed commission to do the panels for the second gallery in the Palais du Luxembourg. It has been said that Rubens was so naïve he failed to realize Cardinal Richelieu would not grant such an order to a man whose diplomatic activity had been directed against the best interests of France, but this could not have been the case.

Rubens' long and varied experience as a diplomat must have convinced him that Richelieu would oppose him. Believing an accomplished fact would be irresistible, however, Rubens went to work on his Henry IV series, and actually completed many superb sketches. Two completed paintings, "Triumphal Entry of Henri IV into Paris" and "The Battle of Ivry," now hang in the Uffizi Gallery. Of the sketches, "Henri IV in Battle" is in a Hamburg collection and "Henri IV at the Battle of St. Martin l'Église" is the property of the Alte Pinakothek, Munich.

Rubens notified the French that he was at work on the enterprise but received no reply from either Richelieu or the Queen Mother. Finally word was sent to him through a quasi-official source that France had signed no contract with him and was not obligated to accept any portion of the Henry IV series.

In a letter to Dupuy, the contents of which Rubens knew would be seen by Richelieu, he maintained an air of hurt bewilderment. Through no fault of his own, he declared, he had lost a fortune in France, and he was convinced that this had been caused by some inexplicable misunderstanding. Hoping to increase the pressure on the cardinal, he added:

> I have said, in general terms, that to meet with so many difficulties at the commencement of this undertaking seems to me inauspicious, for I am deprived of the courage and, to speak truthfully, somewhat disgusted by the innovations and changes to my own prejudice and that of the work itself, whose splendors and

luster will be greatly diminished by these retrenchments.

Here Rubens was referring to the work depicting Henry IV's greatest triumph, which would have graced a wall at the end of the palace gallery. He started the painting but abandoned it when Richelieu refused to rise to his bait. Rubens finally learned, as did so many others, that no one then alive could persuade Richelieu to take action against his own best interests and those of France.

The gamble had been taken, and the painter had lost. At no time would his completed paintings hang in the Palais du Luxembourg, and he finally realized he had done work in vain.

The defeat still rankled late in 1630, when the Archduchess Isabella called him to Brussels in order to bestow an honor on him that restored his dignity and further fattened his already-bulging purse. The regent appointed him to the post of Secretary of the Privy Council of the Netherlands, a position that required no work but paid him an honorarium of three thousand gold crowns per year. The post was honorary, and he would be succeeded in it by his eldest son when he either died or elected to retire.

Rubens was determined to speak the last word in the controversy, and in the autumn of 1630 he finally went to work on yet another commission which had been given him by Louis XIII. The artist had been requested in 1622 to provide twelve tapestry cartoons depicting "The Life of Constantine," and he carried out the order swiftly after his eight-year delay. Louis tried to avoid payment, complaining that the Roman costumes in the cartoons were not authentic, but Rubens, at his best when dealing with kings whose intelligence did not equal his own, suggested that the drawings be submitted to a committee of experts at the Sorbonne.

Louis foolishly agreed, and his own authorities informed him that the costumes were marvels of precise accuracy. The king was forced to pay and, with great reluctance, sent the artist ten thousand gold écus by far the highest price anyone anywhere had ever paid for tapestry designs.

The actual tapestries were woven by the Gobelin company of France, but it is believed that Rubens never saw them. Certainly he did not supervise the making of the tapestries, which ordinarily would have been his responsibility. He stubbornly fulfilled a contract in order to salvage some measure of victory from the ruins of the only major defeat he had ever suffered.

Then, the cartoons completed, he sent a formal letter to Cardinal Richelieu in his capacity as First Minister of France, tendering his resignation from the Henry IV series project. There had been so many complications and difficulties in the preparation of the work, he wrote, that it would not be in his own interest, that of art, or the good of France for him to remain committed to the work.

Richelieu maintained his customary aloof silence and did not deign to reply. But the artist had saved face, at least in his own opinion, and that was all that mattered to him. Apparently it did not occur to him that he had made himself look slightly ridiculous; in his own mind he had demonstrated that not even the rulers of the strongest national power on the Continent could trifle with him.

Then, having dismissed the matter from his mind, Peter Paul Rubens turned to something far more important. At the age of fifty-three he fell madly in love with a girl less than one-third his age.

XIX

Hélène Fourment, the youngest of Daniel Fourment's eleven children, was sixteen years of age in 1630, precisely the same age as Rubens' eldest son. Nevertheless Rubens fell in love with her, blithely disregarding the fact that she was the youngest sister of Suzanne Fourment, who had been his mistress. His old friend, Daniel, may have been surprised when Rubens requested the girl's hand in marriage, but the father gave his consent in spite of the difference in the ages of the bride and groom. Rubens waived a dowry, of course, since his wife would become one of the first ladies of Europe, the mate of an enormously wealthy artist whose genius was universally recognized.

The marriage ceremony was held on December 6, 1630, at the Church of St.-Jacques in Antwerp, and few people other than the groom and the father of the bride were pleased. The marriage brought a storm of criticism down on Rubens' head, and the good burghers of Antwerp were scandalized. But the happy artist blithely ignored the comments, writing to Moretus, who was in London on business, that they grew out of the jealousy of the widows of Antwerp who had set their caps for him in vain.

Hélène Fourment was a pretty, immature blonde with blue eyes and the generously endowed figure that posterity associates with the name of Peter Paul Rubens. Her femininity was pronounced, but even her husband's most idealized portraits of her—and he painted scores of them—did not reveal more than average intelligence.

The wildly infatuated Rubens immediately used his bride as his favorite model and even managed to include her in many of his larger works. He obviously gloried in her figure and repeatedly painted her in the nude, showing no reluctance to let the whole world see his wife unclad. In fact, he was fascinated by her nudity, again and again calling the attention of posterity to the fact that he, a middle-aged man who was overweight and suffering from rheumatism, had won a marital prize of such splendor.

In spite of the head-shaking and tongue-wagging that occupied the ladies of Antwerp and their solidly respectable husbands, the shy and quiet Hélène made Rubens a remarkably good wife. Once she became accustomed to his art-filled palace she became an efficient domestic manager, running the household so smoothly that Philip Rubens the younger pays her lavish compliments in the *Vita Rubenii*. She was on the best of terms with him, his sister, and both of Rubens' own sons, having been their playmate since earliest childhood.

Apparently she posed in the nude for her husband without protest, although someone with her family training and Church-sponsored education may have suffered guilt and embarrassment. Perhaps she consoled herself with the thought that Rubens' genius was enabling her to share his immortality. The paintings themselves were among the most lavishly Baroque Rubens had ever painted, and he made no secret of his adoration, his work displaying a luminous intensity that has caused posterity to share his admiration of the girl.

The marriage was deliriously happy from the outset, in spite of the many obvious odds against it, and Rubens and his wife confounded their critics. Hélène bore her husband five children: Claire-Jeanne, who was baptized on January 18, 1632; François, baptized on July 12, 1633; Isabella-Hélène, who bore the names of both of Rubens' wives, baptized on May 3, 1635; Peter Paul, baptized on April 1, 1639; and Constance-Albertine, who was born almost nine months after her father's death and was baptized on February 3, 1641.

There was ample room in the house for all of the children, and Rubens spent his most ecstatically happy years with Hélène, their children, his sons by his first marriage, and the nephew and niece he had adopted. Even though he was a twice-ennobled diplomat and had won recognition among the literate people of the world as the greatest painter of his age, he was still a Flemish bourgeois at heart and found his greatest joys in the simple pleasures of hearth and home, surrounded by his large and growing immediate family. It was his essential simplicity rather than the many veneers of sophistication he had acquired that was responsible for the purity and depth of his work as an artist.

There can be little doubt that Hélène Fourment was responsible for her husband's rejuvenation as an artist. Such works as "St. George and the Dragon" and "The Life of Constantine" clearly reflected the artist's experience but lacked the fire that so long had been one of Rubens' principal characteristics. It had begun to appear that his best work was behind him, that he was gradually and gracefully slipping into the twilight of his career. Now, suddenly, all that was changed.

The revitalization of Rubens was little short of astonishing. He brought to his work not only the sure touch of a veteran who knew precisely what he was doing, but he came to life again in ways that were spectacular. His charming paintings were more charming than ever before, a perfect example being the portrait of Hélène, his young son Nicolas, and himself strolling in the courtyard garden. His major works reflected his demonic energy and almost limitless imagination.

His new vitality was seen in all of his works, but there could be little doubt that Hélène was ever-present in his thoughts. In the romantic "Garden of Love," all ten of the young women in the painting were based on the artist's wife and her many sisters. She was all things to him, mistress as well as wife, and he made certain the world understood his feelings for her.

Art authorities have been unable to assign the precise dates when various portraits of Hélène were painted. One of the most renowned, showing her nude to the waist, with a fur throw wrapped around the lower portion of her body, probably was painted during the earlier years of their marriage, and was inspired by a Titian that was similar. Now in the Kunsthistorisches Museum, Vienna, it was seen by virtually no one until Rubens had died. He kept it in his bedchamber, which was rearranged so that the painting caught the light in a way that suited him, and not even relatives were permitted to enter that room.

The most famous of the paintings of Hélène, now in the Louvre, shows her with three of her children; their approximate ages indicates that the work was done in 1637 or thereabouts. She had gained weight, to be sure, but was still beautiful, and, in Rubens' eyes, at least, she possessed a luminous quality. Critics have said that in none of his studies of Hélène did he probe deeply, that she seemed to be lacking in soul, but it may be that he portrayed her to the fullest extent possible.

Her infatuated husband was satisfied with the qualities

she brought to their marriage. Apparently she was a mistress who gave him complete physical satisfaction, she managed his house in ways that suited him, and she was a good mother and stepmother. He had not required more in his marriage to Isabella Brandt, and even better established now, he needed only what she gave.

In view of his overwhelming love for her it is surprising to discover that Rubens' marriage to Hélène in no way diluted or was allowed to interfere with his still greater ambitions. Late in December, 1630, the illness of the Spanish ambassador to England made it necessary to appoint a successor, and the Duke of Olivarez suggested Rubens for the post. Philip IV usually accepted the recommendations of his First Minister without cavil, but in this instance he was wary. The artist's paintings continued to occupy too much of his time and effort, and the king believed he should be offered the position on a temporary basis pending the appointment of another permanent envoy.

Olivarez communicated with Rubens in a frank letter that explained the nature of the offer and the reasons for it. Rubens' reply was equally candid: He would accept the ambassadorship on a permanent basis, he declared, but had encountered too many difficulties when acting as temporary ambassador to serve in that capacity again.

It is not in the least surprising that he rejected the offer of a temporary post since he had learned from his experience, even though he would have leaped at the offer a few years earlier. What is astonishing is that he was willing to give up his career as a painter for a number of years in order to accept a permanent diplomatic assignment. It can only be assumed that he felt he had no more worlds to conquer as an artist, while a permanent ambassadorship would enable him to climb to a still higher rung on the ladder in his career as a diplomat.

Hélène, who loved her magnificent home and reveled in

the homage paid to her as one of the first ladies of Flanders, must have been relieved when her husband decided to remain in Antwerp. At the same time she must have realized that at any time he might be tempted by the offer of an attractive diplomatic post.

Such an offer came much sooner than anyone anticipated and was precipitated by a new internal crisis in France. Marie de' Medici, a constitutionally quarrelsome woman who was incapable of maintaining good relations with anyone, had a falling out with Cardinal Richelieu, now the complete master of France, who held all of the country's power in his patrician hand.

Marie tried to defy him, but her plot had been discovered, and royal troops, including the famous regiment of household musketeers, surrounded the Palais du Luxembourg. Richelieu stopped short of entering the palace and apprehending her, but the Queen Mother knew she would be arrested the moment she left the palace grounds. Obviously it was necessary for her to obtain a safe-conduct visa, leave France, and go into exile.

Marie smuggled a letter out of the country to the Archduchess Isabella, requesting refuge in Brussels and asking that the arrangements for her departure be made by a trusted diplomat. As her representative, she wrote, she wanted Don Peter Paul Rubens, a man she knew well and one in whom she had complete faith. As William Shakespeare had observed less than a generation earlier, kings and queens sometimes had faulty memories.

The regent was a soft-hearted woman who believed it was her Christian duty to accept Marie's request, and she immediately sent for Rubens in order to acquaint him with the project and obtain his consent. He went to Brussels with Hélène, who was presented at court wearing a magnificent brocaded gown and all of the jewelry her infatuated husband had given her. The seventeen-year-old girl must have resembled a seventeenth-century version of an over-decorated Christmas tree, but if anyone at the regent's court regarded her appearance as slightly absurd, he kept his opinion to himself.

Even though Marie de' Medici's treatment of Rubens had been shoddy, he was delighted to accept the offer, willing to make the sacrifice of being separated for a short time from his adored bride. Certainly he was motivated in part by the opportunity to even the score with Cardinal Richelieu, whom he well may have regarded as the real villain in the Henry IV fiasco.

On July 26, 1631, Rubens received his official appointment as special ambassador of the Archduchess Isabella and departed at once for Paris, accompanied by a large suite. Richelieu, who had ignored so many of the letters the artist had sent him regarding his own project, could not refuse to see him now. They held intensive discussions for a period of almost two weeks, with Rubens shuttling back and forth between the Palais du Luxembourg and the Louvre, where the cardinal made his office.

Since Richelieu could not refuse to permit Marie de' Medici the right to go safely into exile without incurring the ill will of the Vatican, Spain, and the Italian states, he gave in with good grace. The real victor, of course, was Marie herself, but Rubens shared in her triumph. He escorted her to Brussels, where they arrived late in the day on August 12. The people of the city lined the streets as the Queen Mother of France and the artist-diplomat rode in an open carriage to the regent's palace, and Rubens was greeted with the cheers usually reserved for conquering heroes. It was one of his happiest hours.

The following month an even greater honor awaited him. In mid-September Marie de' Medici came to Antwerp for the express purpose of publicly expressing her thanks to the man who had saved her from imprisonment and disgrace.

There was no finer home in the city than Rubens' house, and she and her large entourage stayed overnight under the roof of the flattered painter and his dazed bride.

Gifts were presented to the host and hostess, after the fashion of visiting royalty. Rubens received a box of chased gold, lined with sandalwood, and according to a rumor which he never deigned to verify or deny, it was filled with gold écus. Marie presented Hélène Fourment Rubens with a magnificent diamond ring, a reminder of the fact that, thanks to Rubens' skill as a diplomat, she had been permitted to take her priceless jewelry collection into exile with her.

Rubens was not to be outdone and responded as though he himself had royal blood. It pleased him to make a gracious presentation of "several small paintings" to Her Majesty, and each of her ladies and gentlemen received a little Greek or Roman statue or some other artifact of the ancients. The painter must have derived a great deal of pleasure from his own gestures, particularly from the knowledge that his paintings were worth more than Marie's gold and diamond ring.

A French historian who was a member of the Queen Mother's party made a comment worthy of note, writing, "Her Majesty received great pleasure from her contemplation of the living wonder of his paintings, whose colors Admiration herself must have mixed, since the onlooker never tires of praising their perfection and beauty." Not even kings and queens owned works of art as awe-inspiring as those which filled the home of the middle-class painter who now dealt with royalty as his equals.

Madrid failed to approve of what the regent had done; Philip IV believed, with considerable justification, that Richelieu was being unnecessarily antagonized. Rubens supported the stand taken by the archduchess and sent a long report to the Duke of Olivarez that is significant because, for the first time, he removed his mask and allowed his own emotions to take precedence over his self-controlled calm. In private correspondence he had hinted that he disliked France. Now his seething hatred of Richelieu caused him to write a remarkable communication in which he even abandoned his lifelong stand in favor of universal peace.

The policies of France, he declared, were so ruinous to her own welfare that he could not resist hoping "a large number of Frenchmen will perish, and in this way that cruel nation will be weakened. Even if it were necessary to disburse new subsidies, I believe the King's wealth could not be better used for the benefit of our stability and security than in encouraging a civil war in France."

Madrid had no intention of precipitating a new conflict with her powerful neighbor and rejected the advice. Rubens recovered his equilibrium after his uncharacteristic outburst had relieved his tensions, and immediately thereafter he again resumed his customary stance, pleading for peace and urging the reunion of Flanders and the Brabant with the independent Netherlands on a voluntary basis.

Times were changing rapidly, however, and Madrid was entertaining new ideas of its own. The Archduchess Isabella, for more than forty years an influence on the side of peace, was elderly and ailing, her own authority was slipping, and Philip IV took matters into his own hands, launching, late in 1631, an unprovoked attack on the Netherlands in the hope that he could subdue the former province of his ancestors by force of arms.

The unexpected war created chaos in Flanders, and Antwerp was particularly hard hit. The port was closed, the international trade that was the lifeblood of the city ebbed away, and the community suffered a major depression.

Only Peter Paul Rubens, whose income no longer depended on wealthy Flemish merchants and the Flemish Church, escaped unscathed.

The regent was horrified by Madrid's rash action and, rallying what little remained of her strength, sent Rubens on a fact-finding tour of Flanders and the Brabant. His purpose was to prove that the people deplored the war and longed for the restoration of permanent peace. Once he provided this data, the Archduchess Isabella intended to send it to Madrid in the hope that King Philip could be persuaded to change his mind and withdraw his troops.

The report was duly dispatched but had no effect on the course of the war. What the regent and Rubens could not accomplish, however, the liberty-loving Dutch did alone. They put up such a firm resistance to the Spanish invader that Philip and Olivarez belatedly realized the war would cost more than it was worth, particularly as the English might come to the aid of the Netherlands and precipitate another general war.

The regent herself was authorized to treat with the Dutch and arrange a peace, authority having been placed in her hands again so Madrid would not lose face. She promptly named Peter Paul Rubens as her principal negotiator. It was her last official act; she died on December 1, 1632.

Rubens attended her funeral in Brussels, grieving for the enlightened woman who had been his protectress and friend for a quarter of a century. Then, after spending only a few days at home, he set out for The Hague, intending to cross the border under a flag of truce. To his astonishment and humiliation the Dutch army would not grant him a safe-conduct pass and turned him away, closing the frontier to him.

Suffering the worst rebuff of his life, he hurried back to Brussels, where he learned that the States-General, the parliament of the Netherlands, had rejected him as a negotiator and declared him *persona non grata* in their country. He was not a representative of Flanders and the Brabant, the Dutch declared, but was the secret agent of Madrid, masquerading as a Flemish diplomat. As proof, The Hague offered evidence that was difficult to counter. Rubens had served as a negotiator with France on Spain's behalf, had been ennobled by the king of Spain, and had represented Madrid as temporary ambassador to England. A man who was this prejudiced in Spain's favor, the States-General insisted, was incapable of speaking with the voice of Flanders and the Brabant, and peace could be made only by a "true Fleming" whose patriotism was unblemished.

The war went on, and the refusal to accept Rubens as a negotiator created new confusion that prolonged the conflict. Meanwhile a dejected Peter Paul Rubens returned to Antwerp, the victim of his own ambition. Throughout his entire life he had wanted the Low Countries reunited under one flag, with self-rule and justice guaranteed for all, but his dreams were destroyed and he was marked as the culprit responsible for the continuation of the war.

Not only was the stand of the Dutch grossly unfair, he believed, but he had been branded as a traitor to Flanders. To complete his humiliation, he was convinced, his usefulness as a diplomat had come to an end. His Antwerp neighbors, blaming him for the failure of the truce, snubbed him in the streets, and Hélène was in tears because no citizen of Flanders would visit her home or extend a social invitation to her husband.

Rubens had suffered the worst blow he had ever been forced to endure, and as a consequence he was compelled to reevaluate his life and goals. The process was long and painful, and the vanity of the proud man was shredded. He found a measure of solace in the love of his wife and children, but that was not enough for a man who had enjoyed the applause of all Europe. How could he rebuild his life and regain his reputation? Rubens searched desperately for the answers.

XX During the early months of 1633 Peter Paul Rubens wrestled unaided with his great problem. His own experience, combined with all he had seen and heard throughout his lifetime, caused him to realize that anyone who elected to dwell in the fire of international politics was certain to be burned by the flames. On the other hand his work as a painter had never been better. In 1630, soon after his marriage, the Archduchess Isabella had commissioned a large work, the "Ildefonso Altarpiece," for the high altar of the Church of St.-Jacques-sur-Coudenberg in Brussels. This luminous, Baroque triptych, its side panels containing portraits of Albert and Isabella, now in Vienna's Kunsthistorisches Museum, was already being hailed as one of his greatest masterpieces.

His labors as a diplomat had already won him two titles and greater honor than a member of the middle class had any real right to expect. And he realized fully, perhaps for the first time, that these efforts alone had not been responsible for the standing he had won as a diplomat. Kings and queens had paid homage to him because he stood alone as an artist. So, making a decision that would put posterity forever in his debt, he gave up his career as an ambassador for the powerful monarchs of his time and planned to devote the rest of his life to his first love.

For a long time he shared the decision with no one but his intimates, wanting the talk about the Dutch rebuff to die away first, so that he could not be accused of retreating in the face of determined opposition. Not until early December, 1634, did he write to Peiresc to tell his old friend that he intended to spend his remaining years on earth as an artist, a husband, and a father. His many triumphs and few failures as a diplomat were behind him, he had traveled far more than had most men of his time, and he was content to remain in the lovely, comfortable home he had made for himself.

Certainly he realized his position in the world was unique for a member of the bourgeoisie. Neighbors might be suffering because of the war, Antwerp's bankers and merchants might be forced into bankruptcy, but the demand for paintings by Peter Paul Rubens was even greater than it had been, and he could command any price for his work.

Several of his more prominent works, among them "Angelica and the Hermit," a serene triptych called "The Holy Family under an Apple Tree" and many of his portraits and nudes of Hélène date from the period immediately following his momentous decision. He had lost none of his energy, daring, or concentrated fury; never had his eye for color been truer or his touch more delicate.

Other major works followed in quick succession. There was his sensual, superb "Diana Bathing," now in the Boymans-van Beuningen Museum, Rotterdam; on its heels came an "Adoration of the Magi," now at King's College, Cambridge; this was followed by the "Garden of Love," now in the Prado, and "Virgin and Saints," now in the Museum of Toledo, Ohio, which he painted on the order of the Augustinians of Malines. The fathers paid for this painting by collecting alms and obtaining a contribution from the tanners' guild, so Rubens charged them only six hundred and twenty gold florins, a price about one-third of his usual fee at this stage of his career.

Next, and he may have worked on this intermittently, was a decoration for the great banquet hall in Whitehall Palace, London, which Charles I had ordered when Rubens had last been in London. It was a vast scheme, and Rubens divided the ceiling into five major portions, on which he placed three huge paintings and two smaller ones. These paintings rank among Rubens' finest works, possibly because he felt close to King Charles, whose company he enjoyed, and did his best to please the British monarch. The main sections were "The Union of England and Scotland," the magnificent "Apotheosis of James I," and the "Blessings of the Government of James I."

Rarely, if ever, had Rubens done more impressive work. He probably finished the paintings at some time in 1634, and they were installed in the winter of 1636. But he did not go to London to supervise this operation, which would have been customary. Instead he sent the paintings, along with detailed instructions to those whom he charged with responsibility for installation. In a letter to Peiresc he confided that he did not make the journey himself because he had "conceived a horror of courts." King Charles paid him the largest fee he had ever received: According to the agreement, Rubens was to be given a total of three thousand pounds, payable in four installments; Charles was so pleased with the finished product that he sent Rubens an additional bonus of two thousand pounds.

The "Adoration of the Magi," another of his masterworks, was painted to adorn the high altar of the Church of the Dames Blanches in Louvain. Only the sharpest eye could detect a faint muting of the earlier passions; perhaps he was gentler now, even a trifle calmer, but his love for Hélène continued to rule him. She could be found, in one guise or another, in virtually every major painting.

Never had Rubens known a time of greater personal happiness, and it is ironic that Antwerp was suffering as she had not done since the terrible time of the "Spanish fury." In his work, certainly, Rubens seems unaware of the tragedy that surrounded the peaceful island that was his home. He continued to collect paintings and statues with the same acquisitive fervor he had shown all of his mature life, and his home was one of the wonders of the age.

Not even the arrival of the new regent, the Cardinal-Infante Don Ferdinand, brother of Philip IV, early in 1635, caused him to change his mind and become a part-time diplomat again. As Secretary of the Privy Council he was responsible for the regent's reception, and he discharged his obligations, writing to Peiresc that he was so busy he had to carve time for his own work.

Don Ferdinand came to Antwerp in April, 1635, and Rubens mobilized the entire membership of the Guild of St. Luke to honor him. New paintings and sculptures were everywhere in the city, where gay decorations hid the poverty of the people. Rubens himself painted two large works for the occasion, but they were perfunctory, perhaps because Don Ferdinand had accomplished nothing of consequence in his young life. Rubens was required to perform, and he did what was expected of him. Neither he nor any of his colleagues provided paintings or sculptures of consequence for the occasion.

One additional painting by Rubens for the celebration is noteworthy, both as a work of art and because of its extraordinary subject, which had no place in the reception. He called it "Business Deserting Antwerp," and its grim theme called the attention of the new regent to the city's plight. All that is really important is that Rubens finally showed an awareness of his city's struggles. He sympathized with his fellow townsmen but could do little or nothing to alleviate their unfortunate situation.

Don Ferdinand had become acquainted with the artist during Rubens' stay in Madrid, and in a public gesture of confidence he renewed Rubens' appointment as Secretary of the Privy Council. This move actually was unnecessary, as the painter already held the post for the duration of his lifetime. It was interpreted by contemporaries, probably correctly, as an invitation to return to diplomatic service. There were few men of stature in Flanders and the Brabant who displayed even token enthusiasm for the most unpopular war ever waged in the Low Countries, and the new regent needed all the help he could get.

He didn't get it from Rubens. When Don Ferdinand arrived in Antwerp, Rubens—the head of the reception committee—was confined to his bed with an attack of rheumatism that was either real or diplomatic, a question that has remained unanswered down to the present day. The regent promptly demonstrated that he, too, could be a diplomat and called on Rubens at his home. The gesture was intended as a mark of respect, and the people of Antwerp were flattered, but some of the old resentment against the painter flared up again. Was he a Fleming, or was he an imitation Spaniard? Not even his painting, "Business Deserting Antwerp," could restore him to public favor, and the people apparently misinterpreted Don Ferdinand's visit to him.

In May, 1635, Hélène gave birth to her third child, Isabella-Hélène, and the following month Rubens bought a new house in the Brabant. For many years he had owned a small country house on a lake north of Antwerp, which he used for brief periods of rest, but this purchase was intended for a far different purpose.

The painter and his family moved from his beloved Antwerp to the new house, a magnificent mansion located in the little town of Elewijt, a short distance from Brussels. A dwelling worthy of a great and powerful lord, it was a medieval castle that had been modernized and rebuilt over a period of several centuries. Guarded by high walls and higher turrets, the place lay in the center of rolling, green fields and pleasant woods, and the whole was surrounded by a medieval moat.

It was a dwelling in keeping with Rubens' great stature as a painter and retired diplomat, and it was far enough removed from Antwerp so that he and his family could escape the displays of antagonism on the part of his fellow citizens. He did not sell the Maison Rubens in the city, but henceforth he considered the great mansion, known as Steen, as his primary home. By purchasing it, he also acquired the title, Seigneur du Steen—which was formally approved by the new regent—and Rubens was so proud of it that the title was used in the carving on the top line of his tombstone.

Thanks to his purchase, he had the isolation he had long wanted. Antwerp criticized him, calling him a coward and accusing him of running away, but in his own mind he had no real choice. His concept of dignity made it impossible for him to reply to attacks on his past political activities. Certainly he knew that he was in no way personally responsible for the prolongation of the unpopular war, but the demands of diplomatic precedent, which required him to remain silent about his previous work, prevented him from explaining in detail that he had always been devoted to the cause of peace. He saw no reason why his children should be made to suffer for his supposed errors, which were no more than the product of inflamed Flemish imagination, and he moved away from the center of disturbance.

He threw himself into the task of decorating his mammoth new home with the same fervor he had so long displayed in the adornment of his old house. He also painted a large number of landscapes of Steen and its surroundings; these works were among the first landscapes he had painted, and like all of his other work, they demonstrated his total mastery of the medium. He refused to sell any of these paintings but used them as decorations in Steen's many rooms.

One possible project fascinated him. The great hall of the castle was enormous, and Rubens wrote to Peiresc that he was tempted to paint it. After all, Michelangelo's frescoes decorated the Sistine Chapel, and the ceiling of the banquet hall in Whitehall was his own handiwork. He could not forget, either, that among the marvels of the age were his panels in the Palais du Luxembourg. He contemplated the project for several years, even making a number of preliminary drawings, but eventually his own good sense prevailed. He had been paid a fortune for his other projects but wouldn't receive a copper for the decoration of Steen. Too professional in his outlook to do that much work without a fee, he reluctantly abandoned the idea.

In 1636 Rubens received an official appointment as court painter to the new regent, but he was not surprised. Don Ferdinand would have appeared ludicrous if he had offered the position to a lesser artist. Rubens graciously accepted and received an annual fee of two thousand gold florins— an outrageous sum, but one in keeping with his great stature.

A minor controversy still surrounds an incident that took place in 1636 during one of Rubens' many visits to the regent's palace. The Secretary of the Privy Council was closeted alone with Don Ferdinand for several hours, and he hastily departed for home when he emerged. Don Ferdinand was out of sorts for the rest of the day, and it was apparent that Rubens had rejected a major request.

The nature of that request has never been clarified, but

it is assumed that the Cardinal-Infante wanted the painter to resume his former career as a diplomat and that Rubens had refused. Only a man of his standing and stubborn nature would have dared to turn down one of the most powerful men in Europe, but it seems that Rubens was adamant. He was enjoying life to the full at Steen with his wife and children, he was painting regularly, and if he was turning out fewer works than in his most productive years, his current paintings proved he had lost none of his power and fire. He literally had no reason to become a diplomat again.

On the contrary, he had good reason to mistrust the impetuous, spoiled Cardinal-Prince, and events proved he was right. Richelieu signed an agreement with the Dutch, and Don Ferdinand did not wait to learn the precise terms of the treaty, which might or might not have had an effect on the progress of the war. Instead, he personally led a column of troops into the field and captured the city of Trier, which was under French protection in accordance with a special treaty made by Henry IV.

The sacred honor of Henry IV's son had been sullied, and Richelieu immediately declared war on Spain in the name of Louis XIII. Always one to act with dispatch after making a decision, Richelieu sent troops to invade Luxembourg; this corps joined forces with a Dutch army, and for the first time since the beginning of the war the Brabant itself was invaded.

Bishop Antoine Triest, Rubens' good friend, placed himself at the head of a peace party and was determined to open negotiations, first with The Hague and then with Paris. The movement gained such strength that the besieged Cardinal-Infante did not dare to oppose the scheme; had he done so the Brabant well might have revolted.

Rubens visited Brussels regularly during this period, and it was rumored that he would be sent to The Hague as the principal commissioner representing the regent. According to a report sent to Richelieu by one of his spies in Paris, Rubens' two sons by his first marriage would accompany him as secretaries.

According to Rubens himself, attempts were made to persuade him to become a negotiator. But he remembered the Dutch rebuff a few years earlier and kept his promise to himself by refusing. He wrote to Peiresc that he knew from the outset that there would be difficulties because Richelieu, his personal enemy, opposed the granting of a passport that would have enabled him to enter Holland. So, he wrote, he had "at once contrived to waste time on purpose, seeking every means of avoiding involvement." He added: "Since, besides this, there was no lack of people anxious to obtain such a mission, I have been able to save my peace of mind, and, thank God, here I am quietly at home."

In other words, it appears that Rubens might have been willing to make the personal sacrifice had he thought he could make a significant contribution to the cause of peace. But he knew the Dutch were already opposed to him, and Richelieu's machinations against him gave him the escape he wanted.

Some authorities do not agree with this interpretation; they believe that Rubens was anxious to become a negotiator and merely pretended otherwise when the opposition to his appointment was too great. It is possible, of course, that this account is accurate, but no concrete evidence has ever been found to substantiate it, and in view of the determination Rubens expressed so frequently in his correspondence, when he swore again and again that he had retired from the political arena, his own version must be accepted.

In spite of the war and the personal crisis that caused Rubens to move from Antwerp to his castle in the Brabant, he painted some of his greatest works in 1635 and 1636, when he was fifty-nine years of age. His imagination, his power, and his perfection of execution were undiminished.

One of these works is the sketch for a painting that was never done and probably was intended for a Benedictine church. Called "The Miracles of St. Benedict," it illustrates a legend in the life of the saint and is considered by many authorities to be one of the most moving of Rubens' paintings. Delacroix was so excited by this work that he painted his own version of it in 1841, and the two paintings today hang side by side in the Royal Museums of Belgium in Brussels.

The new version of "The Carrying of the Cross" was commissioned in 1634 for the high altar of the church in the abbey of Afflighem. Rubens painted it two years later; the delay was caused by the artist's realization, after paying a visit to the church, that the dimensions in his first sketch were inaccurate. He went home, prepared a second sketch, and then followed it. These sketches are in the Rijksmuseum, Amsterdam, and the State Museum, Copenhagen. In the painting itself Rubens once again demonstrated the dynamic vitality that had been ever-present in his younger days. The real miracle of his work is that he never lost his almost superhuman powers of intensity and sweep, depth and tumultuous action.

The third of his superb paintings during these years was the "Martyrdom of St. Lévin" painted for the Jesuit church in Ghent and now the property of the Royal Museums in Brussels. The subject matter, the torture and murder of the saint, is horrifying, and Rubens' Baroque execution, exquisite in detail, is brilliant. By this time the bulk of his life's work was behind him, but rarely had he done better. His hand was still steady, his eye remained keen, and his larger-than-life imagination was undiminished. A return to the political arena might have sapped his strength and robbed the world of irreplaceable masterpieces. His marriage to Hélène Fourment and his move from turbulent Antwerp to the castle far removed from reminders of war were at least partly responsible for the outpouring of a genius unique in the long history of art.

It was during this time that Bishop Triest paid Rubens the greatest compliment the Fleming had ever been accorded. "This great man," the prelate declared, "stands on a summit only one other is fit to share with him, Michelangelo." Such comments pleased Rubens, naturally, but the satisfaction of his vanity was not enough for him. He needed the hard knowledge that he had achieved what he had set out to do, and when Peiresc wrote to him, telling him the bishop's remark, the artist replied with unfeigned calm:

> I myself long have seen the similarity of my work and that of Michelangelo. Our feelings are not the same and our techniques are different, but we think in the same, large terms, I because of the inspiration he provided me. When I thought of his courage I forced myself to become as courageous. If we are to be judged in the same breath in the future, as men now living so judge us, it is because I, like Michelangelo, am consumed with a love of life, a consuming passion for the human experience on every level, from the lowest to the highest.

This remarkable statement is one of the few in which Rubens judged his own work. His objectivity is surprising, as is his lack of passion. He evaluates himself as critically as he does Michelangelo, and when he stands apart, weighing Rubens the artist, he is drained of vanity. He recognized the intrinsic worth of the body of his lifework and was ready to be judged accordingly. If other men coupled his name with that of Michelangelo, the greatest of the Renaissance Italians, he accepted the tribute because he knew he deserved it.

At no time in his life did he boast of his work as an artist.

Only when trying to achieve greater recognition as a diplomat did he push, nudge, and insinuate. It well might be argued that Rubens the man was as vulnerable as Rubens the diplomat. He married two women in his lifetime, both much younger than he, endowed with physical beauty and personal warmth but lacking in the intellect he prized in his male friends and in himself.

As a painter he refused to rest, even after he passed his sixtieth birthday. In all probability he was psychically incapable of sitting back and accepting praise for what he had already done. New challenges continued to beckon, and in the autumn of 1636 one of the greatest and most demanding confronted him.

XXI

In an age when the monarchs of all major European nations claimed they ruled by divine right, neither the Bourbons of France nor the Stuarts of England were quite as autocratic as the Hapsburgs, and in that family the Spanish branch was even more arrogant than the Austrian. Enormously wealthy, they were indifferent to the plight of their poverty-stricken subjects; self-indulgent and a law unto themselves, they reveled in a luxury beyond the grasp of even the richest potentates in other lands.

Philip IV had inherited more than thirty palaces, castles, and country homes, but he had something of a mania for real estate and purchased a dozen more homes for himself. Each of these dwellings had to be decorated in a style suitable to his extravagant tastes, and the dwelling that was his favorite, a hunting lodge near Madrid called Torre de la Parada, required special attention. A small palace of twenty-five rooms, with outbuildings for guests, others for servants, a special kitchen complex, and barracks to house the half-regiment of household troops who accompanied the king wherever he went, Torre de la Parada had been a rustic retreat when Peter Paul Rubens had visited it in the company of Philip IV during the artist's last visit to Spain.

Now, in 1636, Philip was dissatisfied with the simplicity of his lodge and wanted it redecorated in keeping with his exalted opinion of himself and his family. Only the greatest of living painters could accomplish what he had in mind, and he sent a special emissary to Steen with an extraordinary offer: He wanted Rubens to paint enough pictures to fill the walls of every one of the twenty-five rooms in the main lodge building. In return the artist could name his own fee.

Rubens spent a week or two studying the blueprints the royal emissary had so thoughtfully provided and estimated that the task would require the painting of at least one hundred and ten pictures, possibly more. The task was so overwhelming that a man approaching his sixtieth birthday was foolish to contemplate the undertaking, but it was impossible for Rubens to resist the challenge.

He realized, however, that the project would require years of hard labor, and he countered the offer with a proposition of his own: He would supervise the entire task and would paint some of the pictures himself, but he wanted the right to call in other painters from Antwerp to assist him. All of the work, he promised, would be done in what was now known as the "Rubens style," and he offered a guarantee that the paintings would form what he called a grand harmony.

In the autumn of 1636 the deal was made. Rubens promised to supply King Philip with a total of one hundred and twelve paintings. In return the artist requested a fee of eighty thousand gold crowns, by far the largest sum ever paid for any collection of paintings; Philip agreed. It has been estimated that the master kept approximately one-third to one-half of the total, paying the rest to his fellow artists. He also pledged to use his best efforts to complete

218

the work as rapidly as possible, but, wisely, he set no precise date.

In the late autumn of 1636 Rubens went to Antwerp and laid the offer before his colleagues in the Guild of St. Luke. A number of them responded, agreeing to participate. The best known was Jordaens; others included Jacques-Pierre Gouwi, Cornelis Schut, Cornelis de Vos, Theodor van Thulden, Erasmus Quellin, Pieter Symons, and Thomas Villeboirts. It is known that there were still more who took part in the preparation of the paintings, but many of the works were subsequently scattered, and the artists' identities can only be guessed.

Rubens returned to his own studio and, displaying his customary enthusiasm for a major project, began to make drawings, most of which he distributed to his colleagues. But he was interrupted in December or January by the worst attack of rheumatism he had yet suffered and was totally incapacitated. The anxious Philip bombarded his brother with inquiries about the progress of the overall scheme, and Rubens tried to conceal his ailment but was forced to admit to the regent that he could not work.

Late in January, 1637, Don Ferdinand reported to his brother that Rubens had lost none of his enthusiasm for the task, but added, "I fear greatly that the work may be lagging, for Rubens gives no precise answers to my many questions. He promises only that he and the other painters will not lose an hour of time."

Other difficulties cropped up and delayed the project. In spite of the esteem in which the other painters held Rubens, they themselves were men of spirit who resented too close supervision, and there were frequent clashes of temperament. Although many had served as Rubens' apprentices and assistants in years past, all were masters in their own right and had to be treated accordingly. Cliques formed and re-formed within the group, feuds raged, and the painters not only resisted the attempts of Rubens to coordinate their efforts but fought so much among themselves that he had to make frequent trips to Antwerp to quench the fires.

It appeared that, for the first time in his long career, Peter Paul Rubens would be unable to fulfill a contractual obligation. The correspondence of numerous contemporaries reveals that many people wondered why he had accepted such a difficult assignment. He didn't need the money, even though the fee was huge, and the very nature of the project made it impossible for him to enhance his own prestige.

As usual, Rubens kept his own counsel, and his motives can only be guessed. In the light of his lifelong approach to his work, however, it can be assumed that he took on the task simply because it was so difficult. He thrived on challenges, which kept him young and vigorous. Other men in their sixties—living in an age when preventive medicine and geriatrics were unknown—were considered very old. But the husband of a young wife, the father of small children, apparently felt obligated to prove to the world that he alone had discovered the fountain of youth. His ultimate success was not the least of the miracles Rubens performed.

On January 21, 1638, Don Ferdinand sent a special courier to Madrid to inform King Philip that the mammoth project was finally completed. The paintings were assembled at Steen, where Rubens put his own touch on those that failed to live up to his exacting standards; then he supervised the packing and crating, and the paintings went off to Madrid by special caravan, guarded by a battalion of Spanish troops.

The location of only a few of the completed paintings is known today. The Torre de la Parada was sacked in 1710, and those of its contents that were not destroyed were scattered and never recovered. Almost all that remains of Rubens' work consists of his sketches, among them "The Triumph of the Milky Way," the "Fall of Phaeton," "Cupid on a Dolphin," "The Fall of Icarus," and "Aurora and Cephalus." Some are now in the Royal Museums in Brussels, others are in the Prado, and still others are known to be in various private collections.

Unless the finished paintings were vastly superior to the sketches, which is unlikely, they reveal Rubens in a light-hearted mood, and some critics have even accused him of carelessness in carrying out this assignment. Had these works been accomplished by a lesser artist they would have been regarded as superb, but they cannot be considered among the best that Rubens painted. His mastery of techniques had not lessened and his imagination remained unbridled; it can be argued, too, there there was no diminution of his Baroque spirit. At the same time, however, he did not put his heart into his work. The few finished panels, now in the Prado, reveal an indifference, not evident in the sketches, which was uncharacteristic of Rubens.

Perhaps the project was too great for him to handle, although this is a dubious assumption. It is far more likely that his recurring attacks of rheumatism, which sent him to his bed for days at a time, crippled him to an extent that made it virtually impossible for him to devote his unremitting, best efforts to a project of this magnitude.

All the same, Philip IV could not complain. His hunting lodge was the envy of other kings, he had acquired new works by Rubens, who was turning down other assignments, accepting only what interested him, and the Spanish throne considered its money well spent. Ultimately, of course, just one of the Rubens' sketches would be worth many times the cost to Philip of the entire project.

By late 1637 a distinct change had taken place in the routines that Rubens observed. Even when his health permitted, he no longer worked from dawn to dusk. To an extent he was unable to change the habits of a lifetime and continued to arise at daybreak. But after attending mass in the chapel at Steen, where he was joined by members of his family and his neighbors—since there was no church in the vicinity—he relaxed with Hélène and the children over a leisurely breakfast. In good weather he went out for a canter, accompanied by his elder sons, and only in late morning did he retire to his studio.

One of his routines remained unchanged, and caused many of his contemporaries to regard him as odd. Food was important to the people of the Low Countries, who liked to linger for hours over meals of many courses, but Rubens continued to refrain from eating dinner in the early afternoon. He preferred bread, cheese, and wine, consumed in his studio while he worked on a canvas.

As a rule he stopped work an hour or two before sundown to go off for another ride in the countryside, thoroughly enjoying nature and the changing seasons, which called themselves more to his attention as an artist than they had when he had been younger. Returning to the castle, he played with his younger children for an hour or two before dinner.

The principal meal of the day was served in the baronial dining hall, and visitors to Steen reported that Hélène Fourment set a bountiful table, as her own expanding figure demonstrated. As many as ten to fifteen courses, each accompanied by a different wine, might be served on an ordinary evening, and the menu was even larger when there were guests.

No matter what others ate, Rubens still confined himself to thick soups, which he enjoyed, cold meats, and fruit, which he consumed with small quantities of watered wine. In spite of his titles and wealth his tastes were still bourgeois, and Moretus, in one of his last letters to his old friend, teased him about his liking for dried herring, a staple of every middle-class family's diet in the Low Countries. Rubens continued to gain weight in spite of his abstemiousness, but he did not become as overweight as many of his contemporaries. If the increase in Hélène's girth is any criterion—and her husband continued to paint her regularly, obviously still infatuated—he would have become enormous had his appetite been as great.

His last and best-known self-portrait, painted at some time between 1638 and 1640, reveals him as a heavy-set man with plump hands and wrists, a solid body beneath his ruff and cloak, and a full face. It is his face that attracts the viewer's total attention, and he was still a man of great distinction. His forehead was high beneath his rakishly tilted, broad-brimmed hat; his mustache and beard were trimmed and fashionably short; a typical half-smile appeared on his lips; and his chin still jutted forward as the son of Jan Rubens continued to defy and challenge the world. His eyes were as magnetic as they had been in his younger years, and thanks to his genius they reveal the wisdom born of experience and suffering. They are the eyes of a man who had seen too much to be fooled, a man who walked with pride, knowing what he had accomplished, but there was no arrogance in his expression. He had achieved too much, he was too rich and too renowned to assume a false air of humility, but wealth and fame had not robbed him of his compassion for lesser mortals.

Insofar as his work was concerned, perhaps the greatest change that took place in his later years was in his subject matter. He was still the realist, and knowing that the days of his huge, complicated paintings were behind him, he no longer attempted to do such work. The output of his religious works was virtually at an end, and he refused scores of requests for triptychs and other major works.

He concentrated on what he could do with the greatest of ease—principally landscapes, family portraits, and paintings on the various legends of the ancients that continued to entertain and inspire him. He painted principally for his own amusement, and the last known task he accepted on commission was the enormous project for the Torre de la Parada. That experience taught him a lesson he did not forget. No matter how high the price or how powerful and prominent the prospective purchaser, he politely turned down all requests.

Rubens had become one of the wealthiest men in the Low Countries; and no longer needing an income, in spite of the high cost of maintaining his castle and supporting his still-growing brood of children, he lost all interest in money. The staggering price he charged Philip IV for the Torre de la Parada project was a last gasp, a gesture of defiance that told the world he could still command far more than any other artist in history.

When guests were charmed by his landscapes and offered to buy them, Rubens refused. He was painting them for his own enjoyment and that of his family, Moretus wrote, and Philip Rubens the younger confirmed the fact in the *Vita Rubenii.* His attitude created considerable embarrassment when the Cardinal-Infante paid a visit to Steen in the early summer of 1638, presumably to pay Rubens his huge fee for the Torre de la Parada project. The regent admired two of the artist's lovelier landscapes, "The Winter" and "The Summer," now in the British Royal Collections, and wanted to buy them. Rubens, who was suffering from an attack of rheumatism and consequently was crochety, informed him with some asperity that they were not for sale. Nothing daunted, Don Ferdinand offered him an outrageous sum for them, but the painter repeated his refusal. Other members of the party were silent and shocked, since it was a severe breach of etiquette to refuse a request made by a leading member of the house of Hapsburg's Spanish branch. The few who had ever dared had lost favor at court and thereafter found it in their best interests to move beyond the long Hapsburg reach. But Rubens quickly recovered his diplomatic poise and made the regent a gift of the paintings he had admired. On the surface he appears to have taken the easy way out, but this was not the case. Other nobles and Church prelates soon heard of the incident, since everything the regent said or did soon made the rounds, and the brief affair served as a warning to men of lesser standing that the works of Rubens no longer could be purchased.

Kings, of course, did not consider themselves bound by the rules that applied to lesser men, and in the autumn of 1638 Charles I of England sent the painter a request for "an appropriate work of art" he could give to Queen Henrietta Maria. Whether word of the incident involving the Hapsburg Cardinal-Infante had crossed the Channel to London is not known.

Rubens was consistent and sent back word to the monarch who had made him a baronet to the effect that he was no longer accepting commissions for his work because his poor health made it difficult for him to paint. He was too proud to say he was afraid his rheumatism might cause him to produce inferior work. Again he made the grand gesture, however, and sent Charles, as a gift, one of his most charming landscapes, "The Farm at Laeken," which he had painted at a Flemish property he had recently purchased.

The grateful Charles sent him a purse of five hundred pounds, a truly princely gift. But Rubens was too proud to accept payment under the circumstances. Since it would be an insult to return the money, as he well knew, he spent the entire sum on a magnificent cup which he designed and had made for the monarch by a goldsmith who had worked with him in the past. The mere fact that it had been designed by

Rubens more than doubled its worth, and the clever, graceful gesture cemented his already close relationship with King Charles. Certainly no artist other than Rubens could have dealt with reigning monarchs of major nations as though he were their peer.

XXII The ill health that dogged Rubens in 1637 made him realize that his days were numbered, and he began to put his house in order. As nearly as can be gleaned, the better part of his fortune still consisted of cash, but in 1637 and 1638 he began to invest it as he had in his castle, Steen, by purchasing real estate. In those two years he bought eight or nine properties, including farms in Flanders and the Brabant, a town house in Brussels, and a building in Ghent that housed several shops.

Some of these places were occupied by tenants who paid rent, while others were used by members of his family. Albert, the eldest of his sons, who was now twenty-four years old and would succeed his father as Secretary of the Privy Council, lived in Brussels with his wife. The acting master of the Maison Rubens in Antwerp was Philip Rubens the younger, who had obtained a law degree at Louvain and who devoted the better part of his time to the handling of his uncle's business affairs, an occupation that kept him busy. He had married a year or two earlier and was the father of an infant son named Philip-Peter. Also living in the huge Antwerp mansion were his sister, Claire, recently married to a minor member of the nobility, and Rubens' second son, Nicolas, now twenty years old, who had already become a businessman in the reviving city.

It is difficult to determine exactly how many properties Rubens owned at any given time or to pinpoint their location. Philip the younger was empowered to buy and sell, his uncle having given him the right to deal with the fortune as though it were his own and having paid him a fee for his services in precisely the same manner that great nobles paid their stewards. Young Philip had inherited his father's managerial talents as well as his uncle's business acumen, and Moretus is the authority for the claim, made late in 1638, that he had already increased the value of his uncle's enormous holdings by one-fourth.

With no business worries to occupy or worry him, Rubens was able to husband his failing strength for the decreasing number of pictures he was painting. The mere fact that he continued to work was remarkable, but he was incapable of stopping. His work continued to be even more important to him than Hélène and the children, as much as he loved them.

As nearly as can be gleaned, he forced himself to work whenever his rheumatism permitted, and from the time of his move to Steen until 1639 he painted a number of landscapes, most of them in his Baroque style. It was impossible for Rubens to do less than superb work, and his landscapes compare favorably with the best of those done by his contemporaries.

His "limited" ability to produce a substantial body of work was relative, and he turned out scores of landscapes. The exact number has never been determined, in part because he kept no list of his paintings, and in part because, as usual, he signed a painting only when the spirit moved him. Until modern times "new" landscapes by Rubens were being discovered frequently, and even today such claims are made from time to time.

Among the better known of his landscapes are the golden-hued "Landscape with a Cart at Sundown," now in the Boymans-van Beuningen Museum; "Landscape with Goatherd," today the property of the Pennsylvania Museum, Philadelphia; the bucolic, intensely Baroque "Landscape with a Rainbow," now in the Museum of Valenciennes, which some authorities believe may have been painted a few years earlier. Still others are "Return from the Fields," which hangs today in the Pitti Palace; "Landscape with Shepherds" and the "Château du Steen in Autumn," both the property of London's National Gallery; and "The Park of Steen," which he painted a number of times.

The lyric qualities so prominent in Rubens' other works dominate his landscapes, too. "Landscape with Fowler," now in the Louvre, has been called a perfect example of his love of color, his intense admiration for the epic grandeur of nature. Most landscapes are not regarded as strong, but Rubens could not help expressing his love of life, and there is majesty even in his quiet, rural scenes. Sky and earth, trees, houses, and people form the same balanced, harmonious whole that is so evident in his major works; it has been said that any art lover, including the least experienced, is capable of recognizing even the most tranquil of his landscapes as Rubens' handiwork.

His declining health was a never-ending cause of concern to those who were close to him. In April, 1637, Moretus wrote to a mutual friend in Leyden that Rubens' physical condition had deteriorated and that he was now suffering so intensely from rheumatism that it had become impossible for him to draw sketches of even small, simple subjects. Until that time he had continued to provide Moretus with drawings for the flyleafs and title pages of books, but that activity had come to an end by 1637.

Late in 1637 Cardinal di Bagno, the former Papal Nuncio in Brussels, who had returned to Rome, wrote to Rubens asking him for some tapestry cartoons and telling him he could name his own price. A member of the household who acted as the painter's secretary replied that he begged to be excused for the present, adding: "Rubens has not yet recovered from a long and painful illness, which reduced him to extremity. He is at present convalescent, and hopes to write to you himself when he is able."

The cardinal twice pressed Rubens for the cartoons in 1638 but received no reply. The artist procrastinated, unwilling to reject an order from a good friend who was also a prince of the Church, but by February, 1639, he realized that it would never again be possible for him to make such cartoons. So he scribbled a note to the secretary in his own cramped hand: "I beg of you that you will present to His Eminence that the troubles I suffer in my person, which often take the form of rheumatic gout, not permitting me to manage pen or brush, and taking as their usual seat my right hand, prevent me above all from making drawings on a small scale."

In spite of his disabilities, or perhaps because of them, Rubens painted one of his most renowned works, known as *La Kermesse,* which now hangs in the Louvre. It is a salute to the rural joys of Flemish living and is remarkably similar in spirit to the work of Bruegel the Elder. According to a story that may be apocryphal, Rubens painted the picture in a single day; discovering upon awakening that his hand was free of pain, he hurried to his studio and spent the entire day there, as he had done in earlier years, so that he could take full advantage of his momentary good health. The precise date of the work is unknown: Some authorities believe it was done as early as 1636, while others think he painted it as late as 1638.

La Kermesse is one of the least pretentious of his major

works, although it was done in his usual style and with his customary verve. Rubens may have been thinking of his own early years when he painted the tavern with its open-air tables, cooking utensils, jugs, and numerous other homely, necessary objects. He fills his canvas with human figures, as he had done in so many of his vast religious works, and his people are kissing, hugging, dancing, fighting, quarreling, embracing, laughing, drinking, eating. This was the carefree Flanders of his imagination, and he celebrated the spirit of his fellow countrymen in a manner that has immortalized the Flemings of the seventeenth century.

Rubens continued to work until the very end of his life, and in the period from 1638 to 1640 he produced some of his most glorious paintings. It can only be surmised that he retired to his studio whenever his physical condition permitted him to work, and that on these occasions he displayed the same ferocious concentration that had been the hallmark of the younger Rubens. Most of these major works glorified the amply endowed nudes that posterity has associated with his name.

If Rubens were judged by the volume of work produced by other painters, he could be said to have been fully occupied in the period of 1638–1640, and only when seen in relation to his earlier output is it possible to realize that he did far less. It cannot be overemphasized that, when he worked, his powers were undiminished. He was not an old, feeble, and pain-racked man trying to recapture the mastery of his prime; his skills were as great, his love of life as intense, his admiration of the feminine figure as all-encompassing. He was still the immortal Rubens, one of the great painters of all time, and neither age nor illness could mar his genius.

Two of his finer works of this period, the "Offering to Venus," which was inspired by a Titian he had copied many years earlier in Madrid, and "The Judgment of Paris" are almost pagan in their triumphant worship of the female body. The same can be said of three other works now in the Prado, "Nymphs and Satyrs," "Village Dances," and "The Rape of the Sabines." As in his other celebrations of nudes, however, Rubens remained free of eroticism; conservative seventeenth-century Churchmen might think he had gone a trifle too far in his candor, but they could find nothing in his work that would offend them.

Others might not realize he was faltering from time to time, but his own demand for perfection caused him to see what lesser men could not. In 1638, at the urgent request of a colleague, Sustermans, who was enlarging the gallery of the Medicis in Florence, Rubens roused himself to paint a large picture which he called "The Evils of War." Allowing his symbolism to become rampant, he painted a work filled with minute detail, and when he was finished, he was not satisfied with it, although he could not quite define the cause of his uneasiness.

Perhaps his self-confidence did not desert him. It may be that he was merely demonstrating a new facet of his habitual caution when, for the only time in his career, he authorized another painter to make alterations in his work. If "an accident or my own carelessness makes it necessary," he told Sustermans, "I urge you to repair any errors in color or substance that you might find." Sustermans made no changes, and posterity has discovered no need for them either, although some authorities believe his hand was somewhat less certain.

But two of his last religious works, which he painted at a later date than "The Evils of War," are as vigorous and as pure as the masterpieces of his prime. The sisters of the Convent of Mala Strana in Prague begged him for some paintings done expressly for them, and Rubens did not have the heart to refuse them. There is a hint in the *Vita Rubenii* that he accepted the assignment because it might be his last great challenge. "The Martyrdom of St. Thomas" and "The Miracle of St. Augustine" must be regarded as major works, and they stand on a level with most of his earlier achievements, although they were relatively limited in scope.

The ability to rise above his illness preoccupied Rubens, and he felt compelled to accept yet another commission from Philip IV. In the summer of 1639 he went to work on four new paintings, only two of which he completed unaided. Don Ferdinand thought it unlikely that Rubens was capable of doing any work at all, but the artist continued to work daily, even when his pain was so intense that he was forced to take doses of laudanum, a crude opiate, in order to dull his distress.

It is a final irony that the two paintings he finished have vanished. There is no hint of what might have happened to his "Hercules," and only a sketch for it remains. "The Reconciliation of the Romans and Sabines," subsequently known as "The Sabine Peace," was greatly admired at the Spanish court, and Velásquez later called it "a truly great painting." Posterity has had no chance to make its own judgment because "The Sabine Peace" was destroyed in the fire that swept through the royal palace in Madrid in 1734.

Of the two remaining works, "Perseus and Andromeda" was completed by Jordaens, and "The Rape of the Sabines" was finished by another artist in Antwerp who preferred, as a favor to Rubens, not to make his own identity known.

In the early autumn of 1639 Rubens returned to Antwerp with his family after a long sojourn at Steen. It has been suggested that he knew his end was near and wanted to spend his last days in the city he still considered his own. On September 16 he summoned his notary and made out his will, the contents of which he kept secret. Two weeks later he instructed Philip Rubens the younger to buy and sell no more properties; having already made the necessary dispositions of his estate, he wanted no more changes.

Thereafter his illness became worse, and Don Ferdinand sent his own physicians to Antwerp to take care of the distinguished patient. Other, even more powerful men were alarmed when the news of Rubens' illness reached them: Philip IV sent his personal physician from Madrid to Antwerp, and Charles I dispatched the principal physician on the Whitehall staff.

But these medical men, the most accomplished practitioners of their age, could do nothing to halt the spread of the renowned patient's disease. According to the reports they signed together, rheumatism paralyzed Rubens' hands by the end of February, 1640, and thereafter he was permanently confined to his bed.

On May 27 Rubens knew the end was at hand and dictated some changes in his will, which was resealed. At noon on May 30 he died, surrounded by three generations of his immediate family. According to Philip the younger, who was present, his uncle remained conscious until the end, but it was not the custom of the period to record a dying man's last words. As usual, Peter Paul Rubens spoke for himself; eight and one-half months later Hélène Fourment gave birth to his last child, a daughter.

On June 2 an Antwerp chronicler wrote, "Mr. Rubens died three days ago, and all of Flanders mourns for him. Now Jordaens is the first painter here."

Rubens' body was removed to the Fourment family vault in the Church of St. James late on the day of his death, and thereafter thousands of his fellow citizens, men and women who had scorned him because they had questioned his patriotism, filed past his bier and paid their last respects to him. The funeral was held on June 2.

Two years later Rubens' widow placed one of his masterpieces above his tomb, in accordance with his instructions.

Called "The Madonna and Child Surrounded by Saints," it is believed to be a family portrait, and the face of St. George is said to be that of the painter himself. In all probability the half-naked Mary Magdalene was Hélène Fourment.

Rubens' will explains a great deal about the man and his relationships within his immediate family. Frugal to the last, in spite of his great wealth, he specified that all of his property not otherwise left to individuals be sold, and his estate was so large that the inventory required five years of work by his nephew and the probate court of Antwerp.

His plate of gold and silver and his jewelry were divided in equal shares by Albert and Nicolas, the sons of Isabella Brandt, and by Hélène Fourment and her five children.

Albert inherited his father's library of more than four thousand books, perhaps the largest in Flanders, and Philip the younger received a special bequest for the purchase of books. Albert and Nicolas shared their father's collection of coins and medals. Rubens' two eldest children also received his collection of marble busts and statues.

All of the bric-a-brac was sold; this included collections of shells, plaster copies of sculptures, ivory statuettes, inlaid boxes, and even the globes that Rubens had accumulated when he had developed an enthusiasm for geography. His "astronomical instruments" were sold, as were the contents of his chemical laboratories, but he left his microscopes to Philip the younger. All of his clothes were sold, but the swords—marks of nobility—were left to his sons.

The paintings were in a special category. All family portraits Rubens had painted went to the subjects. In addition the inventory listed more than one hundred of his works, as well as three hundred by other painters. The Venetian school predominated, and included paintings by Titian, Veronese, Tintoretto, Muziano, and Palma. Northern Europe was represented by Dürer, Holbein, Van Eyck, Van der Goes, Key, Metsus, Moro, Floris, Lucas van Leyden, and Jan van Hemmesen. There were thirteen paintings by Bruegel the Elder, most of them landscapes. Rubens had owned one Franz Hals and seventeen small paintings by Hals' pupil, Adriaen Brouwer. Also included were large numbers of works by his own colleagues, among them Van Dyck, Snyders, Jordaens, Jan Bruegel, Wildens, and Van Es.

In addition, Rubens had copied a large number of paintings by other masters, learning by emulating them. There were thirty copies of Titian, twenty-one of them portraits, as well as copies of the elder Bruegel, Raphael, Tintoretto, and Leonardo.

The sale of the paintings brought the estate enormous sums of money. Don Ferdinand paid fifty-two thousand gold florins for one lot, and eight thousand for another. Perhaps sibling rivalry caused Philip IV to pay forty-two thousand florins for one group of paintings and twenty-seven thousand for another. It is symbolic of the high esteem in which Rubens was held that the king paid prices of twelve hundred to eighteen hundred florins each for copies Rubens had made of works by Titian, but paid only four hundred florins for a Titian self-portrait.

Members of other royal families also scrambled for works from the collection. The Prince of Orange, frugal like all men from the Low Countries, acquired a bargain when he bought Rubens' "Silvia" for three hundred florins. By 1642 Charles I of England was occupied by the civil war that would cost him his life, and he had matters other than art on his mind.

Members of Rubens' family purchased a number of paintings for themselves at prices far below the market value. Hélène Fourment bought *Conversation à la Mode* for only one hundred and twenty florins, and Albert paid less for several paintings, but had to spend one thousand two hundred and fifty florins for a large landscape of Steen he particularly admired. The husband of Suzanne Fourment, who may or may not have known that his wife had been Rubens' mistress, bought seven portraits of her that Rubens had painted.

The various parcels of real estate also brought large sums into the estate. Rubens specified in his will that Steen, which he had purchased for one hundred thousand florins, was not to be sold during the lifetime of his widow, to whom he left a half-interest, the other half being left in equal shares to his children. His will authorized the sale of the Antwerp house, but it was so expensive no buyer could be found for the place, so Hélène lived there. Other real estate parcels that were sold included eight small houses, each with a garden, in Antwerp; there were two farms, one at Burght and the other at Zwyndrecht; there was a country estate, Hof van Urssele, which included "a splendid garden and many trees," and an even larger estate outside the village of Eeerckeren, north of Antwerp. Two small farms, both of which were occupied by tenants, were located in the vicinity of Antwerp, and there was another in the Brabant, along with several parcels of land there. In addition, Rubens had owned a larger farm on the Scheldt River near the village of Doel.

Philip the younger had invested his uncle's fortune wisely, and the estate also included forty-seven mortgage deeds, the smallest of them worth four thousand florins and the largest more than fifty-five thousand. But not all of Rubens' money was tied up in investments: Almost seventy thousand florins in gold was found in strongboxes at Steen and the Maison Rubens.

One-third of the cash realized by the estate was left to Hélène Fourment, who overnight became one of the wealthiest women in the Low Countries. Albert, who inherited his father's titles and the post on the Privy Council, received one-third, and the remaining third was divided equally among Hélène's five children, Philip the younger, and Claire. There was no mention in the will of Rubens' brother, Jan-Baptiste, or his family.

The artist remembered a number of people with whom he had enjoyed business or personal dealings, leaving one or more paintings to each of them. This group included Don Francisco de Rochas, a Spanish art lover who had acted as his sales agent on a number of occasions. Among the others were his physicians, Jordaens and a dozen other colleagues, an innkeeper whose company he had enjoyed, and several favored members of his household staff, his valet, his groom, and the mason at Steen.

One special clause in the will indicated that Rubens had entertained secret hopes that one of his sons would follow in his professional footsteps. He had saved many hundreds of his own drawings and, in addition, had lovingly collected drawings by other masters, including many by Michelangelo, Titian, Bruegel the Elder, Veronese, Raphael, Tintoretto, Van Dyck, Velásquez, and a score of other great artists. These sketches, most of them rough, were priceless, but Rubens took great pains to emphasize that they were valuable tools for a painter. In a carefully worded paragraph he left the entire collection either "to one of my sons who may wish to take up the art of painting, or to one of my daughters who marries a painter of reputation."

The great artist erred in his judgments of his children's characters. He had left such a vast fortune that his sons were gentlemen, and none would be forced to work for a living unless he wished; the daughters were ladies, and each would go into marriage with such a handsome dowry that it was inconceivable she would become the wife of anyone other than a nobleman.

Rubens left specific instructions that the collection of drawings should not be sold until the youngest of his children reached the age of eighteen years. But Hélène Fourment and the two sons who were of age, Albert and Nicolas, decided in their collective wisdom that the whole clause was foolish. The drawings were sold.

Hélène Fourment remained a widow for five years. In 1645 she was married for the second time to Jan van Broeckhoven, a well-to-do nobleman and former chief magistrate of Antwerp, who owned a large estate at Bergeyck in Flanders. The Maison Rubens was placed on the market immediately after her remarriage and eventually sold for ninety thousand gold florins.

It would continue to be known as the Maison Rubens, however, and the name of the man who had lived there gained additional luster decade by decade in an increasingly literate Europe and the New World. The centuries have confirmed his immortality, but Rubens himself would not have been surprised or expected otherwise. He was, after all, his own best critic.

Selected Bibliography

AVERMAETE, ROGER, *Rubens and His Times*. Brussels, 1964.

BAZIN, GERMAIN, *Rubens*. Paris, 1951.

BURCKHARDT, L., *Erinnerungen an Rubens*. Basle, 1897–98.

CABANNE, PIERRE, *Rubens*. Paris, 1967.

EVERS, H. G., *Pieter Paul Rubens*. Munich, 1942.

FROMENTIN, L., *Les Maîtres d'Autrefois*. Paris, 1927.

GLUCK, G., *Rubens, Van Dyck und Ihr Kreis*. Vienna, 1933.

JAFFE, M., *Rubens*. London, 1964.

MICHEL, J. F. M., *Histoire de L'Arte de P. P. Rubens*. Brussels, 1771.

MICHELETTI, EMMA, *Rubens*. New York, 1968.

OLDENBOURG, R., *P. P. Rubens*. Berlin, 1922.

ROOSES, M., *Rubens*. Antwerp, 1903.

ROSENBERG, A., *P. P. Rubens, Des Meisters Gemälde*. Stuttgart, 1906.

RUELENS, C., and ROOSES, M., *Correspondance et Documents Épistolaires de P. P. Rubens*. Antwerp, 1887–1909.

SALVINI, R., *La Pittura Fiamminga*. Milan, 1959.

STEPANOW, G. *Rubens*. Milan, 1950.

Index

246

Velásquez and, 187–88
will of, 235, 237–38
work of
    artifact designs, 180–81, 225–26
    artistic approach, 72, 95–96, 115,
        121
    artistic autonomy, 126–29, 152–
        53, 182
    attributed to Van Dyck, 76, 85–
        86, 143–44
    books of, 90, 94
    Caravaggio, influence of, 73, 95,
        115, 139
    engraving, 180
    furniture designs, 138
    El Greco, influence of, 86
    Henry IV Gallery, 161–63, 171–
        73, 174, 189–91, 192
    hunting scenes, 157
    landscapes, 211, 223, 224,
        228–29
    Marie de' Medici Gallery, 167–
        68, 169–71, 174
    Michelangelo, influence of, 77,
        82, 89, 115, 151–52, 156, 215
    mythological studies, 141
    nudes, 182, 194–95, 231, 232
    output, 47, 231
    Raphael, influence of, 122
    secular studies, 156–57
    self-evaluation, 106–7, 215
    self-portraits, 92, 110, 180, 196,
        223
    studio assistants, 130–35
    style, Baroque, 122, 127, 128,
        131, 141, 142, 156, 160
    style, development, 86, 95, 115,
        127, 139
    tapestry cartoons, 160, 183–84,
        191–92, 230
    Titian, influence of, 73, 77, 89,
        115, 231
    Torre de la Parada project, 218–
        21, 224
    See also names of specific paintings
Rubens, Peter Paul (son), 195
Rubens, Philip (brother), 11, 24, 37,
    39, 136
    in Antwerp, 101, 106
    education of, 34–35
    family relations of, 60, 69

letters of, 43, 51, 58, 92, 101
marriage of, 102–3
in Rome with Peter Paul, 73–74,
    86–101
Rubens, Philip (nephew), 136–37,
    227, 235, 238
    as Rubens' property manager, 228,
        233–34
    as source, 41, 48, 63, 66, 92, 111–
        12, 119, 124, 145, 178, 194,
        224, 232
Rubens, Philip-Peter (grand-nephew),
    227
Rudolph II, Emperor, 71, 85
Rye, Ferdinand de, Archbishop, 62

"Sabine Peace, The," 233
St. Ambroise, Claude, Abbé de, 170,
    171
"St. Francis Receiving the Stigmata,"
    141–42
"St. George and the Dragon," 189,
    195
St.-Jean-de-Malines, 115, 157
St. Peter's Church (Rome), 86
"Samson and Delilah," 122
Saxony, Anne of, 13–22, 24, 50
Saxony, Maurice of, 13
Scheiner, Christoph, 125
Schleissheim Museum, 139
Schut, Cornelis, 219
"Silvia," 236
Sigismund, Vladislav, King of Poland,
    173
Sistine Chapel, Vatican, 72, 152, 211
Snyders, Frans, 131, 148, 236
Spain, 11
    England and, 174, 183, 188–89
    Flanders and, 25, 31, 32–33, 104–5
    France and, 174, 183, 212
    Spanish Netherlands and, 3, 11–12,
        25, 161, 168–69, 201–3, 209
Spinola, Ambrogio, Marquis de, 105,
    106
Spinola, Brigida, 85
Spinola, Paolo Agostino, 90
Steen, Castle, 210, 237
    landscapes of, 211, 229, 236–37
Stockholm: National Museum, 140
"Summer, The," 224
"Susanna and the Elders," 140